DIGITAL QUICK GUIDE™

P9-ASA-671

GETTING STARTED WITH ADOBE® PHOTOSHOP® ELEMENTS®

Michelle Perkins

AMHERST MEDIA, INC. ■ BUFFALO, NY

To Carey and Liz, for fun at the Royal Pheasant and adventures yet to come.

Published by:
Amherst Media, Inc.
P.O. Box 586
Buffalo, N.Y. 14226
Fax: 716-874-4508
www.AmherstMedia.com

Publisher: Craig Alesse
Assistant Editor: Barbara A. Lynch-Johnt

ISBN:1-58428-164-2
Library of Congress Card Catalog Number: 2004113080

Printed in Korea.
10 9 8 7 6 5 4 3 2 1

TABLE OF CONTENTS

INTRODUCTION

We've all taken pictures and thought, "If only . . ."—if only Mom's eyes weren't closed, if only there wasn't that ugly light switch on the wall, etc. Believe it or not, professionals face the same problems with badly timed blinks, less-than-desirable backgrounds, problem exposures, etc. So how do they end up with photos that look so good? Well, a lot of it is knowing how to avoid those pesky problems in the first place, but another factor is the ability to fix problems after the fact.

For most pros, the software used to accomplish these post-shoot corrections is Adobe Photoshop. While this is a powerful imaging tool, most nonprofessionals find it either intimidating, too complex, or just plain too expensive. That's where Elements comes in. With it, you'll be able to correct most of the problems that people experience with their images, do basic retouching, and add creative effects that help you make the most of your photos.

This book was written using Adobe Photoshop Elements 3.0 on the Macintosh operating system. If you use the software on a Windows system, you will see some very minor variations between the screen shots in this book and what you see on your screen—nothing too tricky, though!

This book is organized in quick, two-page lessons. These are designed to take you from the basic concepts (like opening an image) to more complicated digital imaging challenges. Each lesson builds on the skills learned in the previous pages, so you will avoid frustration by ensuring you've really mastered each skill before deciding to move on.

To try out the techniques, you will also need some digital images to use as "test subjects." You will be best off using a photographic image. You can use your own digital photos, images from a clip-art collection, or film images you have scanned. You can also download images from this book at no cost from the publisher's web site. To access these images, go to www.Amherst Media.com/downloads.htm, click the link for this book, and enter the password Perk1905. Be sure to read the enclosed PDF file; it contains important information. (You'll need Adobe Acrobat to open this PDF file. If it's not already on your computer, download it for free from www.adobe.com.)

1. ALL ABOUT RESOLUTION

Digital images are made up of dots called pixels. The resolution of an image tells us how close together those dots are (the dots per inch—referred to as the "dpi" of an image). Images with dots that are close together are said to have a "high" resolution (a high number of dots per inch). Images with dots that are far apart are said to have a "low" resolution.

The resolution of an image, to a great degree, determines the apparent quality of the image. High-resolution images tend to look clear and sharp—more like photographs. Low-resolution images tend to look grainy, speckled, and blurry. Does this mean you should always create the highest-resolution image you can? Well, no. The more dots in an image, the more the computer has to remember and move around every time you ask it to do something with those dots. This means it will take longer for the image to open, and performing operations on it will be slower. Because it is bigger, you'll also need lots of space on your hard drive to store a high-resolution image.

■ WHICH RESOLUTION IS RIGHT?

So what should the resolution be? The answer is: only as high as it has to be. The precise number will be determined by what you want to do with the image.

If you want to use it on your web page, you'll select a relatively low resolution—probably 72dpi. This is all that is needed to create an acceptably sharp, clear image on a monitor. Anything more wouldn't make the image look any better and would increase the time the image takes to load.

WHICH IS BIGGER?

Which is bigger, the image on the left or the one on the right? Actually, it all depends on how you look at it. The image on the right definitely covers more space, but both images are made up of the same number of identical dots. In the image on the left, the dots are tightly packed, giving it a high resolution (a high number of dots per inch). In the image on the right, the dots are far apart, giving it a low resolution (low number of dots per inch). In the digital world, how much "space" an image covers makes very little difference. What counts is how many dots (pixels) it is made of. How many pixels your image should have is determined by what you want to do with it.

The resolution your image needs to be depends on how you want to use it. The image on the left is at 300dpi, perfect for printing in a book. The image on the right is at 72dpi. This would look just fine on a web site, but its resolution is too low to look good in print.

If you want to generate a photo-quality print on your inkjet printer, you may want to create a file as large as 700dpi. Check the manual that came with your printer for the resolution it recommends for various print settings.

If you'll be having someone else (like a photo lab) print your image, ask them what they recommend.

■ CHANGING RESOLUTION

Elements will allow you to change the resolution of an image. As nice as this sounds, though, this doesn't take the place of proper planning. Elements is great at moving around existing dots (making them closer together or farther apart) and is even pretty skilled at removing dots (reducing resolution). What it doesn't do well is allow you to turn 50 dots into 500 dots. If you ask it to do this, the program will have to guess where to put these dots and what they should look like. Invariably, it won't guess 100 percent successfully, and your resulting image will appear blurry. You might be able to get away with increasing the resolution by 25 percent—but any more than this and you'll probably not like the results.

■ DON'T JUST GUESS

If you're not sure what resolution you need to create the product you have in mind, find out before you create your file. Don't waste your time making complicated refinements on an image that turns out to be unusable. If you'll be using your image in multiple applications (say you want to make a print but also plan to e-mail the photo to someone), create your image at the largest size you'll need. Make any needed corrections to this large file, save it, then reduce its size and save additional copies of the image for other uses.

2. DIGITAL COLOR MODES

If you ever took an art class (or even played around with watercolors as a kid), you probably know that combining two or more colors creates new colors. For example, combining blue paint and yellow paint makes green paint. In fact, almost all colors are actually combinations of some other colors. The exceptions (the colors you can't create by combining others) are called primary colors. In digital imaging, the set of primary colors that are used to create all the other colors in your image is called the color mode.

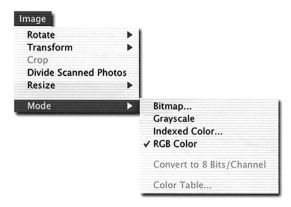

■ RGB MODE

If your image is in the RGB mode (the most commonly used mode in Elements), then all of the colors in that image are made up of some combination of red (R), green (G), and blue (B). It

To switch between color modes, just go to Image>Mode and select the desired mode from the pull-down menu.

may be hard to believe, but by combining just those three colors in slightly different amounts, you can create millions of colors. As a result, this is the best mode for working with color images that you really want to look their best. This is the mode that is normally used for on-screen image viewing (like on the Internet) and most photographic printing (like on an inkjet printer or at a photo lab).

■ GRAYSCALE MODE

A common color mode used in Elements is Grayscale. As you might imagine from the name, all of the colors (well, tones, to be more accurate) in this mode are actually shades of gray—exactly like a black & white photograph. In fact, to quickly convert a color image to a black & white one, you can just switch your image to the Grayscale mode by going to Image>Mode>Grayscale.

■ INDEXED COLOR MODE

This color mode is used for images to be viewed on-screen. It is most useful in situations where perfect image quality is of secondary concern when compared to load time (how long it takes the image to appear on-screen). By limiting the total number of colors in the image to a few hundred (as compared with the millions of colors in RGB), you can get a good-looking image that won't keep viewers of your web site waiting around for your images to load.

■ BITMAP MODE

This mode uses only black and white pixels (no grays). It's more useful for line art than photos, but it can create some interesting effects. To convert to the Bitmap mode, however, your image must first be in the Grayscale mode.

■ A NOTE ON CMYK

The CMYK mode is used for professional printing, but it is not supported by Elements. If you need a CMYK image (say, to appear in a book or magazine), you'll need to use Adobe Photoshop to convert it.

To instantly convert a color image to a black & white one, go to Image> Mode>Grayscale to change to the Grayscale mode.

3. IMAGE FILE FORMATS

Think of the file format as the language in which the digital image is written. It tells applications, like word processing software or web browsers, that your file is a picture (rather than a text file, for example) and how it should handle all the data in the file to display it correctly on the screen. The file format is indicated by a tag (.tif, .jpeg, etc.) added after the file name.

Photoshop
BMP
CompuServe GIF
Photoshop EPS
✓ JPEG
JPEG 2000
PCX
Photoshop PDF
Photoshop 2.0
Photoshop Raw
PICT File
PICT Resource
Pixar
PNG
Scitex CT
Targa
TIFF

Elements is able to read and write a wide variety of file formats.

■ COMPATIBILITY

If you travel to France and try to speak Portuguese to the natives, you'll likely encounter some problems. The same thing can happen with some software applications when you ask them to read a digital file that isn't in their language. Elements is exceptionally multilingual; it "speaks" a wide variety of file formats. Other programs aren't as well educated—many recognize only one or two file formats. If you plan to use your digital image in a program other than Elements, read the software's manual to determine what formats it accepts, then save your image accordingly.

■ COMPRESSION

Some file formats give you the option of reducing the amount of memory your computer will need to store an image. This is called compression.

By reducing the amount of memory required to store an image (i.e., the file size), compression allows more images to be stored in a smaller space and permits them to be transmitted over the Internet more quickly. If this sounds too good to be true, don't worry—it is (mostly). Imagine you crush a soda can. It will take up less space, but it will never look like it did to begin with. With digital compression, the same principle applies—of course, it's rather more sophisticated, and your images won't look as bad as your soda can.

When an image is compressed, equations are applied to arrange the data more efficiently or to remove data that is deemed by the software to be extra-

When an image is enlarged, you can really start to see the difference in quality between JPEG compression (left) and LZW (right).

neous. As a result, your image won't look as good. However, the loss in quality may not be objectionable—or it may be worth it to have an image that loads quickly on your web page.

Two file formats that offer compression are JPEG and TIFF. JPEG offers "lossy" compression, meaning that it removes data and significantly degrades the image. Fortunately, a slider in the JPEG Options window lets you control the degree of compression, so you can compress the file just a little (for better image quality) or a whole lot (when quality isn't as important). The characteristic grid pattern created by JPEG compression (see above) becomes especially apparent when an image is saved and resaved, compressing it each time. For works in progress, this is not a good file format, but it's standard on the Internet because of the small file sizes it produces. TIFF offers "lossless" compression called LZW, which doesn't throw any data out (so the image quality remains better), but it can't compress the image as much.

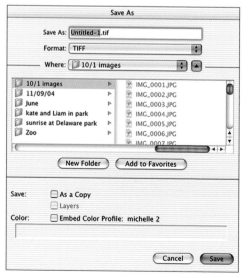

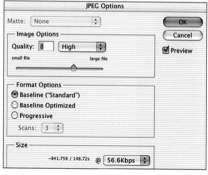

In the TIFF Options window (left), you can select no compression, LZW, ZIP, or JPEG compression. In the JPEG Options window (above), you use the slider at the top of the box to strike the desired balance between file size and image quality. As the file size decreases, so does the image quality.

4. THE WORK AREA

The work area might initially seem a little bit cluttered and overwhelming—there are a lot of menus and boxes! However, the workspace combines similar items into related groupings. This makes navigating it much easier.

■ MENU BAR

The Menu bar runs across the very top of the screen and contains a number of pull-down menus. The following is a brief overview:

File—Open, close, and import files, quit Elements, and more.

Edit—Undo, copy/paste, set preferences for Elements, and more.

Image—Rotate, resize, crop, and make other image adjustments.

Enhance—Adjust the lighting, color, contrast, and more.

Layer—Create, eliminate, or refine layers.

Select—Create, eliminate, or refine selections.

Filter—Select and apply special effects to your image, including artistic looks, sharpening, distortions, and more.

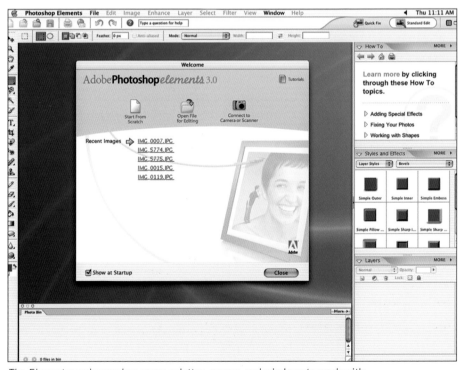

The Elements work area has many palettes, menus, and windows to work with.

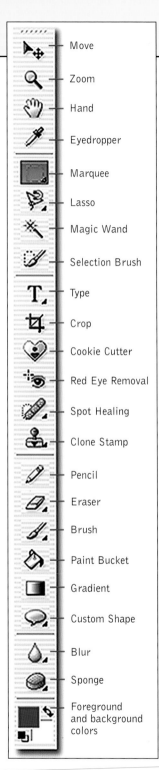

Move

Zoom

Hand

Eyedropper

Marquee

Lasso

Magic Wand

Selection Brush

Type

Crop

Cookie Cutter

Red Eye Removal

Spot Healing

Clone Stamp

Pencil

Eraser

Brush

Paint Bucket

Gradient

Custom Shape

Blur

Sponge

Foreground
and background
colors

Window—Open and close the palettes.

Help—Access to the various help features to rescue you when you're totally stuck.

■ SHORTCUTS BAR

Under the Menu bar is the Shortcuts bar with one-click icons for opening and saving files, printing, and more. There's also a search feature—just type in the term you want to look up, hit Search, and Elements will look for it in its help files.

■ PALETTE BIN

At the far-right side of the screen is the Palette Bin. For more on this, see lesson 6.

■ OPTIONS BAR

Beneath the Shortcuts bar is the Options bar. This bar changes depending on which tool is selected, allowing you to customize the function of that tool to your liking.

■ PALETTES

By default, the free-floating Hints and How To palettes are open on the right side of the screen. To customize the available palettes and their location, see lesson 6.

■ TOOL BAR

At the far left of the screen is the Tool bar. This contains all of the tools you'll need to refine your images—like the Crop tool, Brush tool, Clone Stamp tool, Marquee tool, and more. These will be covered in greater detail later in the book, but to the left is an overview that you may wish to refer back to as you work through the lessons.

5. THE WELCOME SCREEN

The Welcome screen is a nice resource for getting started. Unless you uncheck the "show this screen at startup" box at the bottom of the window, it will appear every time you open Elements. Once you've clicked on any of the option buttons, the Welcome screen will disappear, but you can get it back by going to Window> Welcome.

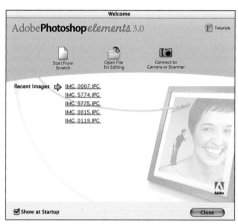

The Welcome screen appears every time you open Elements, giving you quick access to your images.

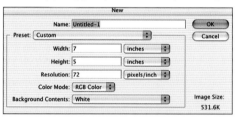

In the New window, you can create a new image, entering exactly the size and resolution you want.

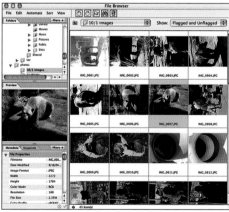

In the File Browser, you can flip through the photos on your computer to find the one you want.

■ START FROM SCRATCH

The top button on the Welcome screen is Start From Scratch. Clicking this gives you the digital equivalent of a blank canvas. On this canvas, you can paint or draw, paste items from other sources (in order to make a collage), etc. When you hit Start From Scratch, the New dialog box shown to the left will appear. In it, you can enter the name of your file, the size you want it to be, the resolution you want (see lesson 1 for more on this), the color mode (see lesson 2 for additional information), and what you'd like the color ("contents") of the background to be.

■ FILE BROWSER

When you hit the Open File for Editing button, the File Browser will appear. In the top left frame of this window, you select a location where you want to look for your image file. All the image files in that area will then be displayed as thumbnails (small images) in the frame on the right. To view a slightly larger version of the image, click on the thumbnail and the image will appear in the center of the left-hand column, with some information about its size, date created, etc., shown in the frame directly below it. Once you've found the image you want to open, double click on it.

■ CONNECT TO CAMERA
OR SCANNER

If you have image-acquisition software for a scanner or digital camera installed on your computer, you can access it by hitting the Connect to Camera or Scanner button on the Welcome screen. Then, simply select your scanner software or dig-

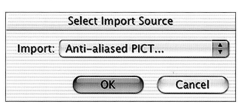

Clicking on Connect to Camera or Scanner activates the Select Import Source window. Choose your scanner or digital camera image acquisition software from the pull-down menu, and it will open automatically.

ital camera image-acquisition software from the pull-down menu in the small window that appears.

■ RECENT IMAGES

Often, you won't be able to finish all the work you want to do on an image in one sitting—or you'll have a flash of inspiration about an image you were just working on. For such situations, the Welcome screen includes a short list of the images you have worked on most recently. Simply select the correct file from this list and go to work.

ANOTHER OPTION

As you use Elements more and more, you'll probably find that you prefer not to use the Welcome screen. To bypass it, unclick the Show at Startup box. You can then create new files by going to File>New, browse for files by going to File>Browse Folders, and connect to your camera or scanner by going to File>Import. Using these commands will open exactly the same windows as hitting the corresponding button on the Welcome screen.

6. WORKING WITH PALETTES

Palettes are small windows that help you enhance your pictures by giving you information about your image or offering you options for modifying it. Elements offers many palettes—and it would be great to be able to have them all visible at once, but unless you work on a system with multiple monitors, this won't leave you much room to view your image. Fortunately, you'll probably find that there are some you use all the time and want displayed prominently. There will be others that you use so rarely that you can just call them up as needed.

You can open any palette by selecting it from the Window pull-down menu. You can also see which palettes are currently open by noting which ones have check marks.

The Palette Bin.

■ THE PALETTES

The individual palettes and their uses will be covered in detail later in the book as we encounter a need for each. For the meantime, however, a quick way to access any of the palettes is to go to the Window pulldown menu and select the palette you want to open from the list. This will make the palette appear on your screen. You can also see which palettes are currently open by noting which items in the Window menu are checked.

■ THE PALETTE BIN

The Palette Bin is located at the right side of the screen. It looks like a series of file folder tabs. To open a palette, just click on the white arrow on the appropriate tab and the palette will drop down.

■ OUT OF THE BIN

To move a palette out of the Palette Bin, simply drag the tab out of the well. This will place the palette in a separate, free-floating window that will remain open on your desktop until you put it away.

Once you have created one free-floating palette in this way, you can drag other tabs into the same window to create a palette group. The names of the palettes in the group will appear at the top of the window as file tabs. You can access the individual palettes by simply clicking on a file tab.

To return a palette to the Palette Bin, simply drag its tab out of the free-floating window and back into the Palette Bin.

When you drag palette tabs out of the Palette Bin, they appear in free-floating palette windows. You can drag more than one palette into each window to group the palettes as you like. Here, the Navigator and Info palettes are in one window.

To reduce the size of a palette in a free-floating window, double click on the file tab.

■ MINIMIZING PALETTES

When a palette is in a free-floating window, you can minimize the window by double clicking on the palette's file tab. This helps save some space on your computer's screen so you can view your image without as much clutter.

■ PALETTE OPTIONS

Many palettes have a drop-down menu, labeled More, at their upper-right corner. From this menu you can select additional options for the function of the palette and create custom settings.

7. VIEWING IMAGES

A lot of the time, you'll be making corrections or changes to your image as a whole—like adjusting the overall color balance in the photo. In these cases, you'll want to see the whole thing from top to bottom and side to side to ensure your changes aren't having any negative effects on some part of the image you can't see.

There will be other times, however, when you'll want to change just a small part of the image—you might want to remove a small blemish on someone's face, for example. In cases like this, it will help you to be able to enlarge just that portion of the image on the screen so that you can see every detail clearly and work as precisely as possible.

There are several ways to control this. To try them out, open an image and practice getting different views of it.

■ ZOOM

When you open Elements, the long vertical window at the upper-left corner of your screen is called the Tool bar. If this is not visible, go to Window>Tools to bring it up.

From the Tool bar, select (by clicking on it) the icon that looks like a magnifying glass (near the bottom-right corner). This is called the Zoom tool.

Position it over the area you want to zoom in on and click one or more times. To zoom out, hold down the Alt/Opt key (a little minus sign will appear on the magnifying glass) and click one or more times.

You can also click and drag over the area that you want to appear on your screen. If you click and drag over a small area, it will be greatly enlarged to fill your screen. If you click and drag over a larger area, it will still jump to fill your screen, but it won't be as greatly enlarged.

■ PERCENTAGE VIEW

At the lower-left corner of your document, you'll see the percentage view. You

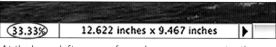

At the lower-left corner of your image, you can enter the percentage at which you want to view your image.

can type in any percentage that you like, enlarging or reducing your view of the document accordingly. Just to the right of the percentage view, you'll see the dimensions of your image—a handy reminder.

◼ VIEW MENU

At the top of the View menu (right) you'll also find several ways to control your image view. The most useful for beginners are: Zoom In and Zoom Out (like the Zoom tool), and Fit on Screen (a quick way to view your entire image).

◼ SCROLLING

Once you have zoomed in, you can use the scroll bars at the right and bottom of the screen to move across the image and view individual areas at a higher magnification.

◼ NAVIGATOR

To view the Navigator window, go to Window>Show Navigator. The percentage at the top-left corner of this window indicates the current view (type over it to change this). You can also move the slider at the top to the right or left to change the size of the area that is being viewed. Similarly, clicking on the "minus" magnifying glass zooms out, while clicking on the "plus" one zooms in. A red box indicates the area that is currently visible on the screen. Once you have zoomed in to the desired enlargement, you can simply click and drag the red box over the area that you want to see displayed in your main window. In the three sequential views of the polar-bear image to the right, you can see how this works.

View

New Window for IMG_5774.JPG

Zoom In	⌘=
Zoom Out	⌘-
Fit on Screen	⌘0
Actual Pixels	⌥⌘0
Print Size	
Selection	⌘H
Rulers	⌘R
Grid	
Annotations	
✓ Snap to Grid	

8. CORRECTING MISTAKES

Yes, you're going to make mistakes from time to time. You'll apply the wrong effect (or realize that the intended one makes the image look really bad). Here's what to do.

■ EDIT>UNDO

If you notice right away that you don't like what you just did, go to Edit> Undo. This will reverse the last thing you did, but *only* the last thing. If you make three brush strokes before noticing you used the wrong color, going to Edit>Undo will only reverse the third stroke; the first and second will remain.

If you go to Edit>Undo, and then immediately return to the Edit pull-down menu, you'll see that Undo has changed to Redo. This lets you toggle between what the image looked like with and without your last change.

■ UNDO HISTORY

Since the Edit>Undo command can only undo the very last thing you did, what happens if you realize you made a terrible mistake three steps back?

The Undo History palette records each change you make to an image. This includes any action that affects the pixels in the image, so it does not include things like zooming in and out, moving palettes around on your screen, etc. It does, however, include each individual brush stroke you might use, and just about anything else you can do to an image. If the Undo History palette is not visible on your desktop, go to Window>Undo History.

In its default setting, the Undo History palette will record only the most recent twenty states (the term for the individual entries in the list of steps in the palette). This helps to save memory, but you can set the number of saved states as high as one hundred by going to Edit>Preferences>General.

In the Undo History palette, states are listed from the top down, so the oldest state of the image is at the top of the list, and the newest one is at the bot-

TRY IT OUT

The example on the facing page uses tools that we'll be getting to shortly, but you can try out the Undo History without them. Open an image and go to Filter>Artistic>Watercolor. Hit OK in the window that appears. Then, look at the Undo History palette. You'll see a new state called Watercolor under the state labeled Open. Clicking on the Open state will undo the Watercolor filter; clicking on Watercolor will redo it.

When an image (top left) is opened, the Undo History palette shows this operation ("Open") as the first state (bottom left). As changes are made to an image, you can track them from top to bottom through the Undo History palette (bottom center). In the image shown here, Auto Color Correction and Levels were used to correct the exposure, then the Type tool was applied. The type was repositioned using the Move tool, and a special effect (called a Style) was applied. The resulting image (top center) was okay, but I wanted to see it again without the type. To do this, I simply clicked on the history state above the Type-tool state (right bottom). This cleared the type and all the effects (top right). I could begin working from here and automatically delete all the following states, or return to any other state and continue working from there.

tom. Each state is listed with the name of the tool or command used to create it, so you can navigate back through the history of an image pretty easily when you need to backtrack.

By clicking on the states in this timeline, you can move back and forth through the history of the image and compare previous versions to the current one, or to undo the last ten steps.

When you select a state, you'll see that the ones below it dim. This indicates that if you continue working from the selected state, these later states will be discarded. Similarly, deleting a state (by clicking on the More menu at the top of the palette and picking Delete) will discard all the states that came after it.

If you accidentally eliminate a set of states you wanted to keep, immediately go to Edit>Undo to restore them.

When you close an image, all of the saved states will be deleted, so be sure you're done with them before you close the image!

9. CHANGING IMAGE SIZE

More often than not, your image won't be exactly the size you want it for your print (or greeting card, or T-shirt, or web site, etc.). In these cases, you'll need to change the image size. If your image will be used in several ways, you may need to resize a few times to get the assortment of sizes you need. Whenever you resize, remember to work from your largest needed file to your smallest. As noted in lesson 1, Elements does a much better job at removing pixels than adding them, so this will help to ensure that your image quality remains as high as possible.

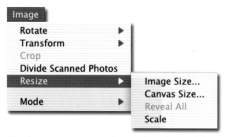

The Image menu contains options for resizing your photographs.

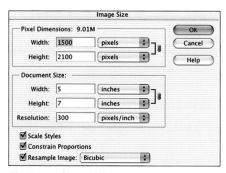

The Image Size window.

■ IMAGE SIZE

Going to Image>Resize>Image Size lets you enter a height, width, and resolution for your image.

At the bottom of the Image Size window, you'll see two very important boxes. This first is the Constrain Proportions box. When this is checked, the original relationship between the height and width of the image will be retained. Unless you intend to distort your photograph, you should always keep this box checked.

The Resample Image box lets you tell Elements whether you want it to add or subtract from the total number of pixels in your image. If this box is not checked, increasing the height and width of your image will decrease the resolution (the existing pixels will be spread out over a greater area). If this box is checked, increasing the height and width of your image will not change the resolution (more pixels will be created to fill the greater area).

■ CANVAS SIZE

Going to Image>Resize>Canvas Size lets you enter additional height and/or width around your image. The color of this extra space will be determined by the background color (see lesson 32). This is a good way to create extra space

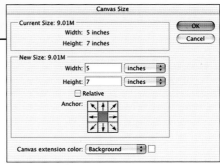

The Canvas Size window.

around a photograph. You can then use the space to add text or other image elements.

In the Canvas Size window, the current width and height of your image are displayed at the top. You can then enter the desired new size and width below that. Pull-down menus let you select your preferred unit of measurement (inches, centimeters, etc.).

At the bottom of the box you can select an anchor position. This determines where the new canvas area will be added around your image. If you leave the anchor (indicated by the dark-gray box) in the center of the grid, the new canvas will be added equally around all sides of your image. If you anchor your image at the bottom left, the new canvas will be added above and to the right of the image.

■ SCALE

Going to Image>Resize>Scale lets you resize your image by clicking and dragging on a bounding box. This technique is covered in detail in lesson 13, where you'll learn how to accomplish several similar transformations.

Increasing the canvas size gives you room to add text around an image.

10. SAVING IMAGES

To save a new image, go to File>Save. The Save As window will then appear. In it, you can set the destination for your new file, enter the name of the file, and select a file format. Then hit OK. With some file formats, a second window will appear—often offering you compression options. Set these as you like. After you have saved a file once, going to File>Save will update that same file with any changes you have made (no window will appear).

■ MAKING A BACKUP

When you are working with digital images, especially those from a digital camera, your original file is essentially your negative—the image as you shot it.

One of the marvelous things about digital imaging is that you can mess around with an image today, and tomorrow (when you decide your grandmother might not find it all that funny to see her head on a monkey), you can just start over from the original file.

For this reason, it's important to make backups of your original images. Ideally, you'll probably want to burn these unaltered images to CD or DVD, ensuring that you won't be able to accidentally save over them and destroy your original.

At the very least, when you start work on a new image, you should save it as a copy. You can do this by going to File>Save As and checking the "As a

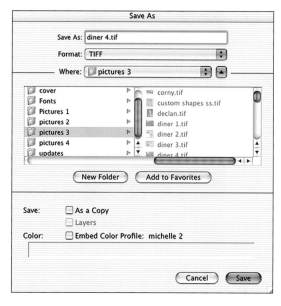

The Save As window lets you specify the location where you want your image saved (from the pull-down menu at the top of the window). Type the name you'd like for your image in the Save As field, and select the desired file format from the Format pull-down menu. You can also choose to save the file as a copy (good for making backups) or to preserve layers in the image (see lesson 25). Advanced users can also embed a color profile for their monitor.

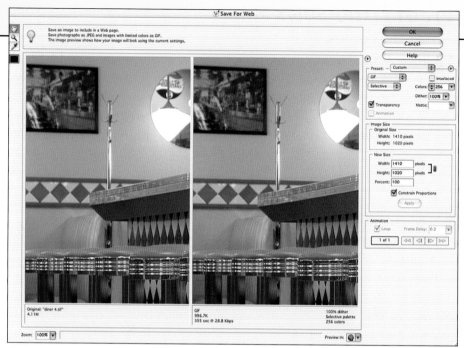

In the Save for Web window, the image on the left is your original, and the one on the right is a preview of the image optimized for the web. Beneath the preview, you can see the total size of the file and the approximate time it will take to load. On the right-hand side of the window, you can adjust the settings to maximize the appearance of the image while minimizing its load time.

Copy" box near the bottom of the window, or simply by selecting a new file name (like "Grandma_backup.tif" or "beachshot_inprogress.tif").

■ SAVE FOR WEB

To save an image to use on the Internet (on a web site or as an e-mail attachment), go to File>Save for Web. From the dialog box, you can select settings and see how long an image will take to load on a viewer's screen, as well as how it will look. You can even preview the image in Microsoft Internet Explorer or Netscape Communicator.

SAVING FOR THE INTERNET

When saving images for use on the Internet, you need to consider image quality (how good the image looks on-screen) and load time (how long it takes to appear on your screen). Typically, load times are reduced by eliminating data—and this reduces the visual quality of the image. There's no one setting that will work with every photo, but if you spend a few seconds playing with the settings in the Save for Web window, you can almost always improve your load time without making too big a sacrifice in image quality.

11. GETTING SOME HELP

While digital imaging is a tremendously exciting and powerful tool for photographers, there's no denying that the learning curve is steep. You'll probably find (at least from time to time) that you've forgotten what a particular tool does or that you can't remember how to adjust a particular setting to get the effect you want—or you might even find yourself totally puzzled as to why something doesn't seem to be working as you thought it would. While it's easy to get frustrated, help is only a click away.

■ SEARCH FROM THE SHORTCUTS BAR

One way to begin your search is by using the Shortcuts bar. To do this, just enter the term or terms you want to look for and click on the question-mark icon. This will open the

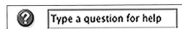

On the right-hand side of the Shortcuts bar, enter a term and hit the question mark to get more information on it.

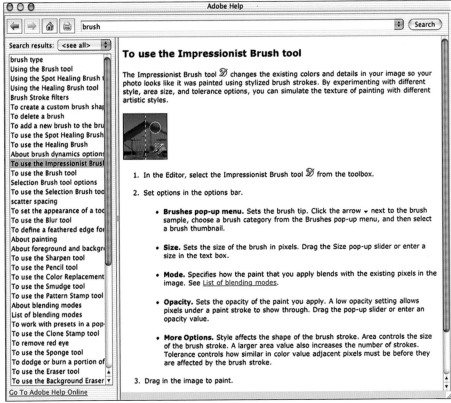

The Elements help files work just like web pages—just click on the links to see the information you're interested in viewing.

Adobe Help window. In the left part of the window, locate the topic that seems most appropriate and click on it.

■ FROM THE HELP MENU

To go directly to the help files, you can also click on Help>Photoshop Elements Help.

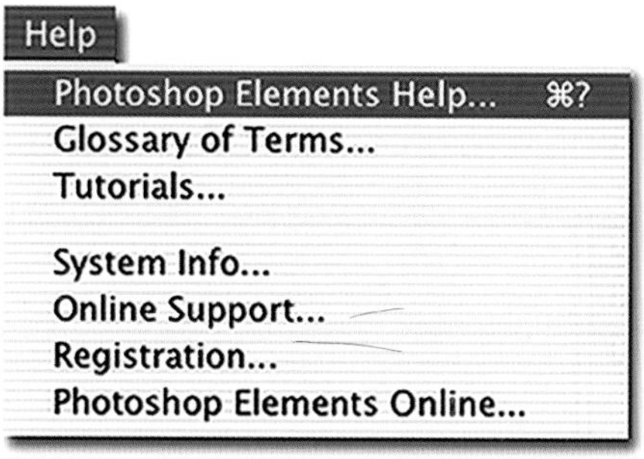

The help files can be quickly accessed from the Help menu.

■ NAVIGATING THE HELP FILES

If you get to the help files via the Shortcuts bar, you'll already have narrowed down the topic that will be displayed. If you open the help files from the Help menu, you'll need to perform a search for the topic you need information on.

To do this, enter your search term at the top of the window and hit Search. A list of links will appear at the left of the window. Scroll through them until you find one that seems likely to answer your question.

You may also find it useful to take advantage of the site index. If the tab for this does not appear above the search-results part of the window, click on the "home" link (the house) at the top of the window. Using the index can sometimes remind you of related topics that will help you refine your search.

TIPS FOR GETTING HELP

Most searches return a large number of search results. If you don't see one that seems to suit your needs, you can add additional terms to narrow your search and make the results more manageable to browse. Also, once you find a topic that looks appropriate, keep your eye open for hyperlinks (underlined blue text) within the entries. Clicking on these will take you directly to related information.

12. DUPLICATE, ROTATE

If you've just scanned an image or just imported an image from your digital camera, it's an extremely good idea to make a duplicate of the original before you begin manipulating it in Elements. You may think you won't make any mistakes—but, like the rest of us, sooner or later you will. And when that mistake is accidentally saving an edited version of an image over the one and only original, it can be pretty frustrating—especially if you wanted to try some other effects on that original before deciding which you liked best.

■ DUPLICATE

To quickly make a backup of your image, you can simply go to File>Duplicate. In the box that appears, you can rename your duplicated image, or use the suggested name (which will be your current file name plus the word "copy"). When you hit the OK button, a duplicate image window will appear in the

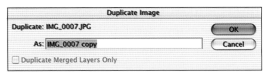

In the Duplicate Image box, you can rename the new image or leave the suggested name (your original image name plus "copy") in place.

Elements workspace. This will be the copy of your original image, and you can begin working on this copy without altering your original.

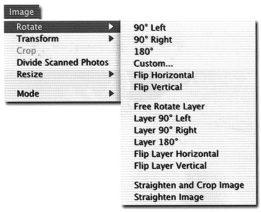

Under the Image menu, you can rotate your image.

■ ROTATE IMAGE

Under Image>Rotate, the top area of the drop-down menu contains options for rotating your image. When you shoot with a digital camera, this is the function you'll use to properly orient your vertical images (the ones you shot with the camera turned on its side). Depending on the image, you can decide whether it needs to be rotated

90 degrees to the left (counterclockwise) or right (clockwise). You can also rotate it 180 degrees—useful if you scanned a photo upside down (or shot it upside down during your trapeze lesson). You can also rotate image layers the same way (see lesson 25 for more on layers).

To take a vertical photo, you tilt your digital camera. When these images are transferred to your computer, they will appear as horizontals, though (above). To get the proper orientation (right), just rotate them 90 degrees to the left or right.

There are some other options for rotating your images—but you probably won't use these quite as often. First, you can select Image>Rotate>Custom and select a specific angle to which you want the image rotated. Extra blank space will be added around your image to accommodate this rotation, and its color will be the color you have set for the background color (see lesson 32).

You can also flip your photographs horizontally or vertically. This can be useful when you are scanning slides or negatives, which are easy to flip the wrong way in the scanner.

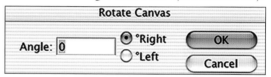

Enter the angle to which you want to rotate the image, note whether it is to the left or right, then hit OK to rotate.

■ STRAIGHTEN AND CROP IMAGE

At the bottom of the Rotate pull-down menu, you can select Straighten and Crop Image or Straighten Image. As the names suggest, these options are designed to automatically crop out extraneous material and correct any perspective problems in your images. With some images, these functions actually work pretty well; with others, they fall well short of the mark. On the next few pages, we'll look at some more precise and controlled ways to accomplish these same tasks in precisely the way you want them for your individual image.

13. TRANSFORMATIONS

When photographing a subject with strong geometric lines, you get the best results when you keep your camera square to the subject—but sometimes this isn't feasible. For example, unless you have an extreme wide-angle lens or can shoot from far away, you normally can't keep your camera square to the subject when photographing a tall building from the ground. This sort of distortion is such a common problem among photographers that Elements has some special tools to help fix it.

■ GETTING STARTED

Transforms can be done to layers (see lesson 25) or selections (see lesson 29). For now, before applying any of the following effects, go to Select>All. You will see a blinking dotted line appear around your entire image, indicating that

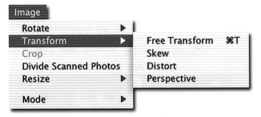

the changes you make will apply to the entire image. For this reason, you should strongly consider working on a duplicate image file (see lesson 12).

From the Image>Transform pull-down menu, you can select several types of transformations.

■ THE BASICS OF TRANSFORMS

After you select an option from the Transform pull-down list, an indicator box with handles (the small boxes at each corner and in the centers of the sides) will appear over your image. If you can't see the edges of your image, reduce your view of the image until you can see your whole image and some gray area around it (see lesson 7). By clicking and dragging on these handles, you will manipulate the image data. Which option you select from the Transform pull-down menu will dictate how you will be allowed to move the handles.

■ FREE TRANSFORM

When you select this option, you will be able to move the sides, top, and bottom of the image in or out and up or down.

■ SKEW

With this option selected, the handles will move only in a straight line in a given direction.

The photo on the left was taken from slightly below and to the left of the window. As a result, the vertical and horizontal lines are all slightly skewed and the window seems distorted. Going to Image>Transform>Distort allowed the image to actually be "undistorted"—resulting in a much better-looking image (right).

■ DISTORT

With the Distort function selected, all of the handles will move freely in every direction.

■ PERSPECTIVE

When you select Perspective, the changes you make are mirrored top to bottom and/or left to right. For example, if you move the bottom-left handle in toward the center of the image, the bottom right handle will also move an equal distance in toward the center of the image. This is a good choice for images where your camera was only tilted in one direction (like up toward a tall building).

■ ACCEPT OR DECLINE

Hit Return to accept the change. If you want to use more than one selection from the Transform menu, you can just choose it without first accepting the existing change (i.e., you can switch back and forth, then click OK to apply the cumulative changes). If you don't like the change, click on another tool from the Tool bar and cancel the transformation when prompted.

14. CROPPING

The Crop tool (see lesson 4) is used to remove extraneous areas from the edges of a photo. This is a great way to improve the look of photographs you didn't have time to frame carefully or ones that you just didn't compose as well as you might have liked.

To crop an image, choose the Crop tool from the Tool bar. Click and drag over the area of your image that you want to keep, then release your mouse button. You don't have to be incredibly precise. At each corner of the crop indicator (the dotted line) you will see small boxes. These are handles that you can click and drag to reshape or reposition the box. (As you get near the edges of the photo, these handles tend to "stick" to the edges. To prevent this, click on the handle you want to drag, then press and hold the Control key while moving the handle.) When the cropped area looks right, hit Enter.

Cropping is a great way to eliminate distractions from an image.

Cropping is a quick way to straighten out a crooked image, but you do lose some pixels in the process. Here, it's not a problem, but it could be more of an issue in other photos.

CROPPING AND RESOLUTION

Cropping reduces the total number of pixels in an image. If you are scanning an image and plan to crop it, you may therefore wish to scan your image at a higher resolution or enlargement to compensate for this reduction. If you are working with an image from a digital camera, the total number of pixels in your image is fixed, so you'll need to determine the final resolution and image size you need and not crop the image to a smaller size than that.

■ STRAIGHTENING IMAGES

The Crop tool can also be used very effectively to straighten a crooked image. Simply click and drag over the image with the Crop tool, then position your mouse over one of the corner handles until the cursor's arrow icon turns into a bent arrow icon. Once you see this, click and rotate the crop indicator as needed. Doing this may cause the edges of the box that indicates the crop area to go outside the edges of the image. If this happens, simply click and drag on each handle to reposition them inside the frame.

■ CROP TOOL OPTIONS

In the Options bar at the top of the screen you can set the final size of the cropped image. This is helpful if, for instance, you specifically want to create a 4"x6" print to frame. Simply enter the desired height, width, and resolution needed before cropping, then click and drag over the image to select just the area you want in your print. The Crop tool will automatically constrain itself to the desired proportions.

Also in the Options bar is a setting for the shield color and opacity. This shield obscures the area you are cropping out, giving you a better idea of what the photo will look like with these areas removed. Leaving it set to black will usually be fine, but you can change the color by clicking on the rectangle to the right of the words Shield Color. You can also adjust the opacity to allow the cropped-out area to be partially visible. To turn off the shield, uncheck the box to the left of Shield Color.

■ SELECT TO CROP

You can also use any of the selection tools (see lesson 29) to crop an image. To do this, select any area of the image, then, with the selection still active, go to Image>Crop.

15. ADJUSTING COLOR

As people who see color all around us every day, we are very savvy about color—we know how things are supposed to look, and when they aren't right, we notice it. The following are some of the challenges to be aware of as you begin working with digital color.

■ COLOR IS SUBJECTIVE

Color is subjective. As a fact of biology, our eyes actively work to preserve the appearance of object colors in changing light, to enhance color differences between objects and their surroundings, and to inform our perception of color using our memories of what objects look like. While this is a marvelous thing in terms of survival (seeing the green snake hiding in the foliage up ahead, etc.), it makes things tricky for people concerned with color accuracy.

■ COLOR VISION

Evolution has decided that as the brain sorts through the data it receives from the eyes, it should try to standardize it to give us the best information by which to survive. As a result, blue objects always look blue—whether we see them under fluorescent, natural, or incandescent light. This is because we don't determine the color of an object in isolation—our perceptions of one color are linked to the colors around it. You can experiment with this by turning on an incandescent light in a room that has previously been lit only by the sun. At first, the light from the bulb will look pretty orange. But gradually, your eyes will compensate for this, and it will begin to look whiter.

■ LUMINOUS SOURCES

When we look at a source of light, our eyes are constantly adjusting to it. That means that the longer you stare at your image on the monitor, the better it sometimes looks. This can make you think it's okay when it's not. The luminous monitor also makes our pupils close down, which can lead us to think an image is darker than it really is.

JUST WALK AWAY

Sometimes you'll reach a point where you aren't sure if your corrections are helping at all. When this happens, it helps to walk away for a little while and relax your eyes. When you return to your image, you'll often be able to see immediately what steps are needed.

Even relatively small variations in color can make a big difference in a photograph—especially where skin tones are concerned.

■ VIEWING AREA

Your eyes will adapt to your monitor no matter what you do, but taking control of your viewing environment can help. Start by selecting a neutral gray for your computer's desktop pattern, since the colors you see around the edges of an image can affect how you perceive the colors in the image. The color of the environment around the monitor can also cast color reflections onto it, so try to keep the area neutral and constant. If possible, place your computer in a room with white or gray walls and position it so that there is no glare on the screen. Try to keep the light levels (and types) in the room constant throughout the day, and from day to day.

16. QUICK FIX

The most basic way to make overall corrections to a digital image is to switch from the Standard Edit mode into the Quick Fix mode. This is done by clicking on Quick Fix at the upper-right corner of the screen. When you do this, some components of the work area will change their function and appearance (as shown in the image below). These changes are designed to give you quick access to simple tools for making the most commonly needed corrections to digital images.

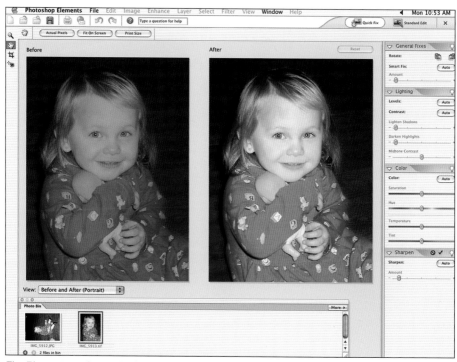

The Elements work area in the Quick Fix mode.

■ IMAGE VIEW

Below your image, the View menu lets you select how you want to preview your results. Being able to see the before and after versions of your photograph simultaneously makes it easy to figure out what changes need to be made. Choose the Portrait setting for vertical images or the Landscape setting for horizontals.

Choose a preview setting from the View menu.

THE PHOTO BIN

The Photo Bin automatically appears at the bottom of the screen in both the Standard and Quick Fix editing modes. From it, you can quickly flip back and forth between any of the image files you currently have open in Elements. While this is a nice feature, you may find that it's actually more helpful to free up space on your screen (giving you  more space to view each image). If that's the case, you can simply close the window by going to Window>Photo Bin (you can make it visible again using the same command).

■ GENERAL FIXES

In the Quick Fix mode, the Palette Bin becomes a set of editing tools. The first category of tool is called General Fixes. Here, you can rotate your image or use the Smart Fix tool to apply automatic corrections to the color and contrast of your image. Use the slider to adjust the amount of correction applied. This may be all you need to do—but if further refinements are needed, you can make additional adjustments using the other Quick Fix tools.

■ LIGHTING

In the Lighting category, you'll find tools for adjusting your image's brightness and contrast. You can click either of the Auto buttons to do this automatically or, for more control, use the sliders to lighten the shadows, darken the highlights, or adjust the midtone contrast. (The midtones are all the colors and tones in your image that are somewhere in between the darkest shadows and lightest highlights.)

■ COLOR

Under Color, you can adjust the color saturation (how vibrant or muted the existing colors are), the hue (changing the colors themselves), the temperature (making the colors warmer [more red] or cooler [more blue]), and the tint (making the colors more magenta or green).

■ SHARPEN

Finally, you can sharpen your image—either automatically or incrementally—using the Amount slider. Be conservative with sharpening; too much can make your image look very bad. For more on sharpening, see lesson 36.

17. AUTOMATIC CORRECTIONS

Getting the tones in your images just right can be tricky. With the automatic image-correction functions in Elements, however, it's often simple to create dramatic improvements.

That's the good news. The bad news is that Elements is, after all, a piece of software—it's not equipped with human vision. To compensate for this shortcoming when making its automatic corrections, it is forced to assume what the image is supposed to look like. Elements assumes, for instance, that you want there to be at least a small very dark area and a small very light area. This is, in general, characteristic of a well-exposed image with good contrast. If you are working with a softly lit photo of a tree in dense fog, however, this assumption isn't going to make your image look very good at all.

The software also makes assumptions about the overall lightness and darkness that an image should have and about how the colors in the image should be balanced. When your images match these assumptions (and many photos actually do—they didn't pull these assumptions out of midair, after all), you are likely to get pretty good results—maybe even great ones—from the auto functions. When your photos don't match these assumptions, however, the results achieved with the auto functions can be pretty scary.

That said, it only takes a couple of seconds to figure out if these methods will give you the results you want, so it's almost always worth giving them a try. Just be prepared to hit Edit>Undo if you aren't happy with the results.

Enhance	
Auto Smart Fix	⌥⌘M
Auto Levels	⇧⌘L
Auto Contrast	⌥⇧⌘L
Auto Color Correction	⇧⌘B
Adjust Smart Fix...	⇧⌘M
Adjust Lighting	▶
Adjust Color	▶

Go to the Enhance pull-down menu to access the auto correction features.

■ AUTO SMART FIX

When you select the Auto Smart Fix Tool, Elements will make any corrections it determines are needed to the overall color and adjust the highlights and shadows (altering the contrast) if necessary.

■ AUTO CONTRAST

The Auto Contrast command, as the name implies, adjusts the contrast of your image—and only the contrast. It will not fix any color problems that might be present in your photograph. If the contrast in the image you are working with seems a little flat or dull but the color looks okay, this would be one strategy you could try.

The original photo (top left) lacked contrast and had a yellow color cast. The Auto Contrast (top right) helped the contrast but not the color. The Auto Levels (bottom left) improved both the color and contrast, taking the image to a sepia tone that is probably close to what the image originally looked like. The Auto Color Correction (bottom right) fixed the contrast and eliminated the color cast, rendering the photo in pure black & white tones.

■ AUTO LEVELS

Auto Levels performs a correction that is similar to Auto Contrast, except that it also affects the color of your image. Theoretically, this should remove any overall color cast—but if your image doesn't have an overall color cast, it might actually add one. Still, this is worth a try for images that need a little more contrast and have an obvious color cast you want to remove.

■ AUTO COLOR CORRECTION

This is the most sophisticated of the three automatic functions—and it works remarkably well on a lot of images. While it sometimes introduces color problems, in many images it will be all you need to get the color and contrast to a point that is quite acceptable.

18. SHADOWS/HIGHLIGHTS

When pros take pictures, they have lighting equipment to perfect each image. For the rest of us, adjusting problematic lighting after the fact can help our images live up to the same high standards. Elements offers two tools that are designed to help photographers address lighting issues.

◼ BACKLIGHTING

One of the most common lighting problems is backlighting—light that comes from behind the subject of the photograph and toward the photographer. This type of lighting causes two exposure problems. First, the background (where the light is strongest) will be overexposed. It will usually lack detail and be too light. Second, the form of the subject will be in shadow, resulting in tones that are too dark. The best solution for this is to use flash (if your camera has a fill-flash setting, this is exactly what it was designed for) to add light on the subject when you are taking the picture.

The Shadows/Highlights command helps you correct lighting problems.

When this is not possible, you can use the Shadows/Highlights command to help create a more pleasing image. You'll get the best results when the difference in brightness between the subject and the background is not extremely high. If the background is washed out to pure white, you probably won't be able to make much of a positive change. If the subject's features are almost impossible to pick out or in extremely deep shadow, you probably won't be able to restore them to a very flattering appearance—but you can always try it and go to Edit>Undo if it doesn't work out!

In the original image, the overall exposure and contrast were fine. However, the shadows were so dark and sharp that they were distracting. Using the Shadows/Highlights command, we can significantly improve the situation.

Darkening the highlights is clearly the wrong approach to this lighting problem—notice how the overall image now looks incorrectly exposed and the colors have shifted in an unnatural way.

Lightening the shadows is a better approach. It made image detail visible in areas where it was hard to see in the original. Some additional tweaking could be used to really refine the image, but this is a good start.

◼ DIRECT SUNLIGHT

Unfortunately, many of our best photo opportunities occur in lighting situations that are less than optimal. A bright, sunny day is a great time for a family picnic or other outing where photos are part of the fun—but bright, midday light actually makes it very *hard* to get good images. The shadows it creates are often very dark and harsh (as you can see in the polar-bear photos in this lesson). Lightening the shadows in this situation can sometimes help salvage a favorite image.

19. BRIGHTNESS/CONTRAST

In most cases, our ideal images will contain a full range of tones (from very dark to very light), where the subject is represented accurately (not too light or too dark). Sometimes, however, the lighting on a scene or subject makes this tricky—or even outright impossible. That's where the Brightness/Contrast tool comes in. When using this tool, remember that the *brightness* of an image refers to its overall lightness or darkness. The *contrast* refers to the difference in brightness between the lightest and darkest tones.

Making adjustments to the brightness and contrast is easy. Go to Enhance>Adjust Lighting>Brightness/Contrast. This will open a dialog box like the ones shown on the facing page. To increase the contrast or brightness, just move the appropriate slider to the right of center; to reduce either setting, move the slider to the left.

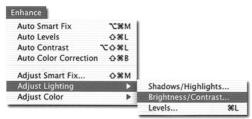

The Shadows/Highlights command helps you correct lighting problems.

Be careful, though! The tool can be overused. If you make an image too bright, too dark, or too contrasty, you will lose detail in some part of that image. This may be acceptable in some cases, but is usually not desirable—so adjust these settings carefully.

To prevent problems, make small, gradual adjustments to the contrast and keep an eye on the darkest and lightest areas of your image. If you adjust the contrast so that it is very high, you'll see that these critical areas will start to lose detail (becoming pure white or pure black). If your goal is to create a natural-looking photograph, this is something you'll generally want to avoid.

In the original image, the overall exposure and contrast are problematic. The image is a bit too dark and the colors look flat and muddy because the contrast is a little bit too low. Using the Brightness/Contrast command can help this image.

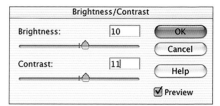

The original photo (facing page) lacked contrast and was somewhat too dark. Adjustments were made in the Brightness/Contrast dialog box (above) to brighten the image and boost its contrast. The resulting image (right) shows a big improvement!

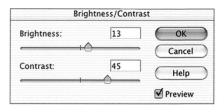

Beginning from the same original photograph as the example at the top of the page, the contrast and brightness were increased much more (above). The result (right) is just not pleasant—there is none of the detail that we'd like to see in a photo. This is especially evident in the highlights and shadows, which are pure white and pure black.

Use your best judgment when adjusting the brightness of the image. Depending on the subject matter, the style of the image, and the look you are going for, the adjustments you decide to make may vary quite widely from image to image.

Two examples (one good, one bad) of the Brightness/Contrast tool in use are shown above.

20. ADJUST COLOR

The Enhance>Adjust Color commands are useful for quick color changes and offer creative possibilities that will add some variety to your images. The following are the most commonly used commands from this group.

■ REMOVE COLOR CAST

Select this to open a dialog box and turn your cursor into an eyedropper. Click on a gray, black, or white tone in the image to remove the color cast.

■ HUE/SATURATION

The Hue/Saturation command lets you select a range of colors from an image (say, all the reds) and adjust them without changing the other colors. To do this, select the color you want to change from the Edit pull-down menu at the top of the dialog box. Making sure that the Preview box is checked, adjust the Hue slider to change the color. The Saturation slider allows you to adjust the intensity of the color. The Lightness slider does just what its name suggests.

With the Colorize feature activated, you can render an image in a monotone color—excellent for creating the look of a sepia-toned image. To do this, click Colorize, then drag the Hue slider to the left or right until you like the color. When using this feature, it is often desirable to slightly reduce the saturation of the new color in the image.

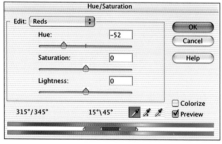

Setting the Edit pull-down menu to red and dragging the Hue slider to the left, the red window frame was changed to purple without affecting the other colors in the image.

■ COLOR VARIATIONS

When you open this tool, a box appears with your "before" image in the top left and eight preview images at the bottom. Simply click on these to accept the change shown in the preview—and you can keep clicking box after box until your image looks just right (or, if you get off track, just click the Reset Image button to start over). Using the buttons at the bot-

This color image was given a sepia look using the Colorize feature in the Hue/Saturation dialog box.

tom left of the box, you can make changes to primarily the highlights, mid-tones, shadows, or the overall saturation. With the slider under these buttons, you can adjust the settings to make big changes with each click or very subtle ones, depending on how you want or need to change your image. When the "after" image at the top right looks the way you want it, hit OK to apply the changes.

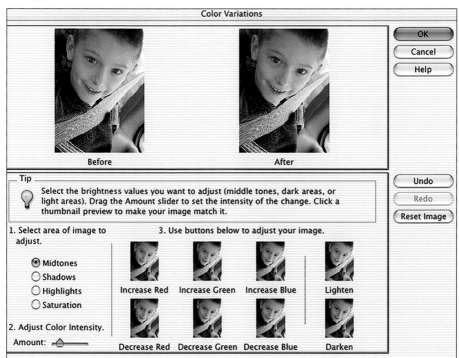

The Color Variations dialog box.

21. A FEW MORE TOOLS

These tools affect the color and/or exposure of your image. The results you'll achieve can be useful and may enhance your creativity. All of these tools can be found under the Filter>Adjustments menu.

■ EQUALIZE

When you apply the Equalize command, Elements makes the brightest tone in the image white and the darkest one black, then evenly redistributes the rest of the pixels in between.

■ GRADIENT MAP

The Gradient Map command uses a blend of colors to map color data over the equivalent tonal range of your image. The dark tones in your image will be

Original image.

Gradient Map filter.

Posterize filter.

Invert filter.

Warming Photo Filter.   Cooling Photo Filter.

replaced by the color at one end of the gradient, while the light tones will be replaced by the color at the other end.

■ INVERT

The Invert command evaluates the tones and colors in an image and then switches them to their opposites—blues become yellow, blacks become white, etc. The resulting image is essentially a negative of the original.

■ POSTERIZE

Posterization reduces the range of tones in an image to a limited number. The resulting images have very little detail. When you access the Posterize command, a dialog box will appear. In this box, the single control option is the number of levels. The lower the levels, the fewer the colors that will be used.

■ THRESHOLD

The Threshold command converts your image into a very high-contrast black & white photo. When you select this, a dialog box appears, and you can adjust a slider to control which tones are black and which are white.

■ PHOTO FILTER

When you click on Adjustments>Photo Filter, a dialog box will appear. From the Filter pull-down list, you can select the name of the filter you want to apply. A wide variety are available from warming (making your image more red) to cooling (making your image more blue). Using the slider at the bottom of the box, you can control the intensity of the effect.

22. LEVELS AND HISTOGRAMS

The color- and exposure-correction tools we've looked at so far offer quick solutions to some problems, but they don't provide much precision. To take control of the colors and tones in your image, you need to master Levels.

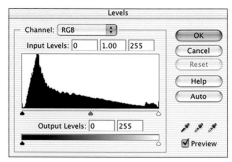

The Levels dialog box.

◼ HISTOGRAMS

When you open the Levels dialog box (Enhance>Adjust Lighting>Levels), the first thing you'll probably notice is a jagged black shape in a white window. This is called a histogram, and it is a graphic representation of the tonal values in your individual image.

◼ ADJUSTING IMAGES

Under the histogram are three triangular sliders. At the left is the black shadow slider, which sits under the area of the histogram that represents dark tones. In the center is the gray midtone slider, under the area of the histogram that represents the midtones. On the right is the white highlight slider, under the highlight area of the histogram. The taller the histogram is above each area, the more tones in the image fall into that tonal range. By clicking and dragging these sliders, you can change the tonal range and contrast of your image. Making small changes, experiment with these to see the effect each slider has. A basic correction is shown on the facing page.

TIPS FOR LEVELS

1. When using Levels, make sure that the Preview box is checked so that you can see the results of your changes.

2. When you like what you see, hit OK—or hit Cancel, if you need to start over.

3. At the top of the box is the Channel menu. There is one channel for each primary color in your image—red, green, and blue—as well as a composite channel for all three (RGB). (See lesson 2 for more on primary colors.) It's the ability to adjust each channel individually (and as much or as little as you want) that makes Levels the most powerful color-correction tool in Elements.

4. Clicking the Auto button does the same thing as hitting Enhance>Auto Levels.

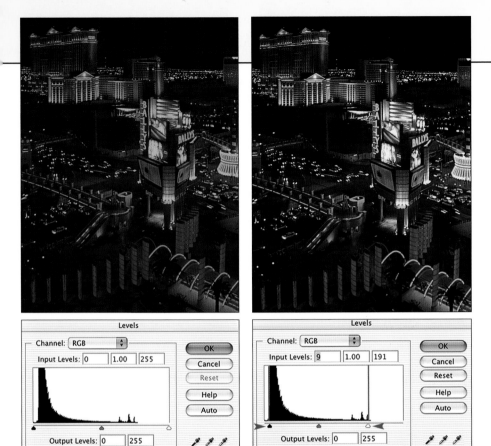

For a basic contrast correction, move the black slider to the right until it is just under the edge of the histogram data. Then, move the white slider to the left until it is just under the edge of the data. For a more advanced correction, use the Channels pull-down menu at the top of the dialog box and perform this same operation in the individual red, green, and blue channels. Be sure to complete all three channels before evaluating the results; the image will shift colors throughout the process, but any color cast and contrast problems will usually be eliminated with the completion of the final step.

◼ EYEDROPPERS

At the bottom right of the dialog box are three eyedroppers. From left to right, these are the Set Black Point eyedropper, the Set Gray Point eyedropper, and the Set White Point eyedropper. To use these, begin with the Set Black Point eyedropper and click on an area of your image that should be pure black. It will be rendered as such, and the other tones in the image will shift accordingly. With the Set White Point eyedropper, click on an area that should be pure white. If an area that should be neutral gray exists in your image, click on it with the Set Gray Point eyedropper. You may find it takes a little experimentation to get the colors just right, but it's a quick and easy process!

23. FILTERS

A filter is a specialized piece of software that runs within Elements and is used to apply a specific effect to an image—we already looked at some simple ones in lesson 21, as a matter of fact. Many filters are packaged with Elements itself, and other filters (from Adobe and other companies) are also available to meet specialized needs.

■ APPLYING FILTERS

You can apply filters using the Filter Gallery (Filter>Filter Gallery). Depending on the filter, this may also open a panel on the right-hand side of the Filter Gallery in which you can customize the filter's settings.

You can also apply filters by going to the Filter pull-down menu at the top of the screen. Pulling this down will reveal several submenu categories that contain the individual filters. Select any filter to apply it. Some will apply immediately, some will open a free-floating dialog box in which you can customize the settings.

While filters can add some very interesting effects, one of the most useful filters is the one used to sharpen images—as you'll see in lesson 36.

In the Filter Gallery, a preview of your image appears in the left frame. In the middle, samples of similar filters are shown (to apply one, just click on the sample picture). In the right frame are sliders and menus you can use to adjust the results you get with each filter. Experiment with these and watch the preview window to see how they affect your image.

Original image.

Pointillize filter.

Lighting Effects filter.

Watercolor filter.

Sumi-e filter.

Spherize filter.

Chalk and Charcoal filter.

Diffuse Glow filter.

Find Edges filter.

24. EFFECTS

Lizard skin! Green slime! Molten lead! Okay, these may not be things you'll use every day, but you have to admit it's tempting.

The effects in Elements work a lot like the filters, but they are significantly more complicated and often involve several steps. Fortunately, all the steps are totally automated, so all you have to do is drag the desired thumbnail icon from the Effects palette (in the Palette Bin) onto your image and watch it go to work.

Some of the effects are designed specifically to work on text (see lesson 34), layers (see lessons 25–26), or selections (see lessons 29–30). When this is the case, you'll see an "T" (for text) across the thumbnail or either "layers" or "selections" in parentheses after the name of the effect. Most of the effects, however, will work on any old image, so give these a try.

From the pull-down menu at the top of the palette you can select to view all of the effects at once or just see select groups, like textures or frames.

In order to accomplish some of these interesting effects, Elements will automatically create layers in your image (these are covered in detail in lessons 25–26). If this causes you problems when you are trying to save or work on your image, just go to Layer>Flatten Image and the layers will be eliminated without changing the appearance of your image.

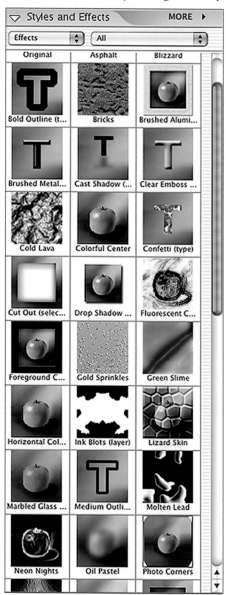

The Effects palette from the Palette Bin. Don't forget to scroll all the way to the bottom of the list to check out all the options!

Original photograph.

Blizzard effect.

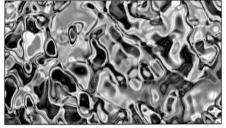

Green Slime effect.

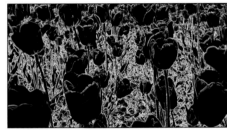

Neon Nights effect.

Ripple Frame effect.

Wild Frame effect.

Colorful Center effect.

Marbled Glass effect.

Oil Pastel effect.

Rubber Stamp effect.

25. THE BASICS OF LAYERS

Layers are like sheets of clear plastic, laid one on top of the other. Each layer can be accessed, worked on, moved, or deleted independently of any other layer. This is great for trying out effects, since you can simply discard the layer if you don't like the results.

■ LAYERS PALETTE

Layers are created, accessed, and manipulated via the Layers palette. If this is not visible on your screen, go to Window>Layers, then look for the palette (see below) in the Palette Bin. The main feature in the Layers palette is the list of layers. These are stacked from bottom to top. The background layer (the photograph you opened or a new image you're going to add to) is at the bottom and the layers that overlay it rise one after another to the top of the palette. While the background layer must remain in the background, you can reorganize the other layers as you like by clicking on the layer (usually to the right of its name) and dragging it into a new position on the list.

■ MAKING LAYERS

When you open an image or create a new image, you'll see only one layer: the background layer.

To create a new, empty layer, go to Layer>New>Layer. Alternately, use the More pull-down menu (at the upper-right corner of the Layers palette) and select New Layer. Doing so will open a dialog box with a blank space to type

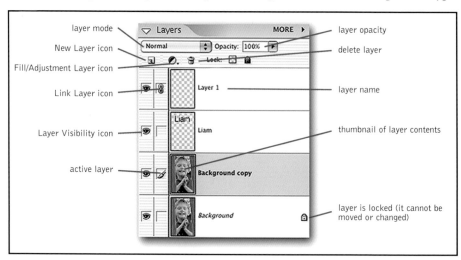

a name for your new layer. If you don't want to name it yourself, Elements will label the new layers sequentially (Layer 1, Layer 2, etc.).

Often, you may want to duplicate an existing layer. To do this, go to the Layers palette and drag the existing layer onto the New Layer icon. Open an image and try this with your background layer.

You can also create a new layer by dragging in a layer from another image. To do this, open two images and position them so both are at least partially visible on the screen. Choose the Move tool (see lesson 4), then click on one image and drag it over the other image.

Another way to create a new layer is to select some or all of an image (see lessons 29–31), then copy (Edit>Copy) and paste (Edit>Paste) it. The pasted area will automatically appear in a new layer.

■ REMOVING LAYERS

To delete a layer, drag it onto the trash can at the top of the palette. This will remove the layer and any data on it. To get rid of all of your layers while preserving the data on them, go to Layer>Flatten Image. This will composite all of the layers down into one—preserving everything you've added. To composite one layer with the one directly below it, select the layer to be composited, then go to Layer>Merge Down. To composite some (not all) of your layers, make invisible (click the eyeball icon off) the ones you want to preserve. Then, click on a visible layer to activate it and go to Layer>Merge Visible.

■ SAVING FILES WITH LAYERS

Because digital images are so malleable, you may find that you want to return to an image several times to make improvements. This makes it a good idea to save a working copy of your image before you do any flattening or merging of layers. By preserving the layers, you'll ensure the widest range of editing options. To save your file with the layers intact go to File>Save As. Then, select the Photoshop (PSD) file format from the pull-down menu, name your image, and hit OK. For many applications (like saving the file as a JPEG to use online), you cannot have layers in your file. In these cases, save a copy with layers (as a PSD), then flatten the image and save a copy of the image in the TIFF or JPEG format.

26. MORE ABOUT LAYERS

To begin playing with some layer settings, you'll need to create an image with layers. To get started, open two images and drag one into the other as described on the previous page. Don't worry if they aren't the same size or look weird together—this is just for practice!

◼ LAYER OPACITY

A layer's opacity determines how transparent it is. To adjust the opacity, click on an overlying layer (not the background) to activate it. Then, at the top of the palette, set the opacity as you like. At 0 percent the layer will be invisible; at 100 percent it will be opaque.

Flower overlays leaf on separate layer.

Flower layer set to 75-percent opacity.

Flower layer set to 35-percent opacity.

◼ LAYER MODES

The layer modes are a predetermined set of instructions for how the layers should interact with each other. To experiment with the layer modes, activate any layer (other than the background layer) with image data on it. Then, use the pull-down menu at the top of the Layers palette to switch its mode.

Flower layer set to Vivid Light mode.

Flower layer set to Exclusion mode.

Flower layer set to Linear Burn mode.

◼ MAKE VISIBLE/INVISIBLE

When you want to work on a layer without being distracted by image elements on other layers, simply make those layers temporarily invisible. To do so, click on the Layer Visibility box (see lesson 25). Doing so will make the eyeball icon disappear, indicating the layer is invisible. To make it visible again, click the Layer Visibility box again.

LAYER MODES

Normal—No change takes place.

Dissolve—Pixels scatter based on their transparency.

Multiply—The mathematical value of the top layer is multiplied with that of the bottom layer(s).

Screen—The mathematical value of the top layer is added to that of the bottom layer(s).

Overlay—Light areas in the top layer are "screened" (see above); dark layers are "multiplied" (see above).

Soft Light—Based on the overlying layer, treats black as burning and white as dodging (see lesson 37).

Hard Light—Very similar to the Overlay mode.

Color Dodge—Similar to both Screen and Lighten, tends to lighten images.

Color Burn—Like Color Dodge, but darkens images.

Darken—Chooses the darkest values of the affected pixels.

Lighten—Chooses the lightest values of the affected pixels.

Difference—Displays the difference between the top and bottom pixels based on their hue and brightness.

Exclusion—Inverts colors in the underlying area based on the lighter areas in the overlying layer.

Hue—Alters the color of the layer without affecting the brightness or saturation.

Saturation—Saturation of upper layer replaces that of lower layer.

Color—Colors of upper layer replace colors of lower layer, while brightness remains constant.

Luminosity—Retains underlying layer's color and saturation while basing brightness on the upper layer.

■ LINKING LAYERS

Often, it's helpful to link layers together. Imagine that (for some reason) you have your subject's body on one layer and her head on another. They are perfectly lined up, but now you want to move them both three inches to the left. You could move them individually and realign them, or—better yet—you could link them. Then, when you move the head, the body will always come along with it (as well it should!).

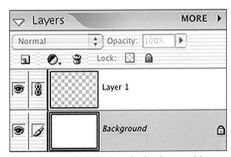

Here, layer 1 is linked to the background layer.

To group two (or more) layers, choose one of the layers and click on it to activate it. Then, click the Link Layer box next to each layer to be linked to the one you selected. A chain will appear, indicating the layer is linked to the layer that is currently active. To unlink any of the layers, click on the chain again and it will disappear.

27. LAYER STYLES

Sometimes you don't want your layers to blend seamlessly with each other. The layer styles will help you create visual definition and add a sense of depth.

Begin with an image that has two or more layers (layer styles cannot be created on a background layer). In the example shown below, a leaf was used as the background and three smaller pictures of various flowers were added. (Hint: The image on the layer where you create the effect should have some free edges [not fill the entire layer edge to edge].)

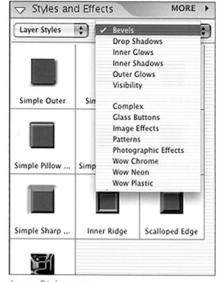

Layer Styles menu.

Drop Shadows layer style set to Low.

Outer Glows layer style set to Fire.

Complex layer style (Chrome) and drop shadow.

Bevel layer style and drop shadow.

DIGITAL SCRAPBOOK PAGES

Because layer styles let you add a "layered" look to your digital images, they work well when creating scrapbook pages that actually look handmade (but take much less time to assemble!). As with traditional scrapbooking, you can still use decorative papers, stamps, and other media—just scan them all first. Once scanned, you can add these elements to your images again and again. Best of all, you can endlessly reposition each item until you get everything just right, then print out the final image and insert it in your scrapbook album. You can even print out multiple copies to make as many duplicate albums as you want. In the image below, you'll see that text can also be incorporated into your page design. Check out lesson 34 for tips on how to do this.

Early Morning in our Backyard

"Flowers are not made
by singing,
'Oh, how beautiful,'
and sitting
in the shade."
—Rudyard Kipling

To apply a layer style, activate the layer to which you want to apply the style (by clicking on it in the Layers palette), then open the Layer Styles palette in the Palette Bin, select an effect, and drag it into the image frame. Notice that there are various groups of layer styles that can be accessed from a pull-down menu on the right-hand side of the palette.

The effects of layer styles vary widely, so experiment with them and keep them in mind for future projects!

28. ADJUSTMENT LAYERS

When you've applied color corrections so far, it's been to the image itself. With adjustment layers, you have more options—and that's always a good thing!

■ WHAT THEY ARE

Adjustment layers are essentially hybrids, combining the features of layers with the functions of the Levels, Brightness/Contrast, Invert, Posterize, and other color-correction commands. There are several important advantages to using these on an adjustment layer. First, because the effects are seen on the image but contained on a discrete layer, you can toss the offending layer in the trash

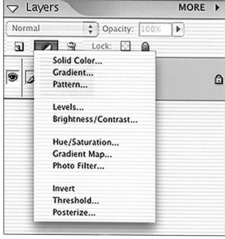

Open any photograph that needs some color correction work.

Click on the Fill/Adjustment Layer icon at the top of the Layers palette and select the tool you want to use.

if it doesn't look right. Second, because the effect is on a layer, you can reduce the opacity of the layer to reduce the impact of the change—a great way to really finesse your image. Third, you can also change the layer mode of the adjustment layer to make it blend with the underlying layer in useful ways. Finally, you can access the tool's settings on this layer again and again—they don't zero out or return to the default settings when you hit OK.

■ CREATING ADJUSTMENT LAYERS

To create a new adjustment layer, identify the layer you want to modify by activating it in the Layers palette. Then, go to Layer>New Adjustment Layer and select the tool you want to use from the menu. Next, you will see the New Layer dialog box. Enter the settings you want (you can change them later in the Layers palette) and hit OK.

Then, the dialog box (if any) for the selected tool will open. These work as described in the previous lessons on individual tools.

To skip the New Layer dialog box, go to the Fill/Adjustment Layer icon at the top of the Layers palette (see lesson 25). Clicking on this reveals a pull-down menu. Select the tool you want from this menu, and the dialog box (if any) for the tool will open up.

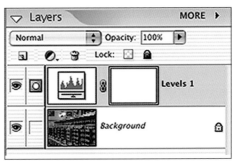

Levels was selected, and this opened the Levels dialog box and created a new adjustment layer.

■ MODIFYING ADJUSTMENT LAYERS

In the Layers palette, adjustment layers look rather unique. On the left is a layer thumbnail with a graphic representation of the tool used on that layer. If you decide you want to change the values you entered in the dialog box for the tool, simply double click on its icon in the layer. This will reopen the box so you can adjust the settings.

Adjusting the Levels removed the color cast, but it seemed to go a little too far; the photo looked cold and uninviting.

To the right of the layer thumbnail is the layer mask. This allows you to define areas where you do not want to apply the change on the layer. To do this, click on the layer mask icon, then select a brush and paint on the image in black, "masking" these areas. As you do so, the

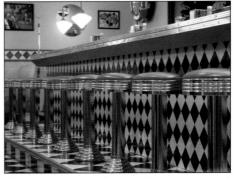

The opacity of the adjustment layer was reduced to 80 percent to restore some of the warmth of the original color balance.

change included on the adjustment layer will be eliminated from the masked areas. To unmask an area (restoring the effect on the adjustment layer), paint over it with white. (See lessons 32 and 33 for tips on painting.)

29. MAKING SELECTIONS

So far, the techniques discussed have been applied to the entire image. The selection tools allow you to isolate individual areas and apply your changes to only those regions. When using selection tools, the areas you have selected are indicated by a flashing dotted black line around the area. Making this line fall exactly where you want it to is the key to making accurate selections. (*Note:* Once you have made a selection, do not click anywhere else on your image with a selection tool unless you want to deactivate [eliminate] your selection. If you accidentally do this, use the Undo Histories to reactivate it.)

■ SELECT ALL

The simplest way to make a selection (of your whole image) is to go to Select> All. Try this just to see what the selection indicator looks like.

■ MARQUEE TOOL

The Marquee tool (see lesson 4) is used to make rectangular or elliptical selections. In the Tool bar, click and hold on the Marquee tool icon to make both options visible. Select the tool that best matches the area you want to select, then click and drag over the desired image area to select it. To select a perfectly square or perfectly round area, press and hold the Shift key, then click and drag over your image.

■ LASSO TOOL

The Lasso tool is used to draw around an irregularly shaped area using a continuous line. This line can be made up of any combination of straight and curved areas. To use it, select the Lasso tool, click on one edge of the area to be selected, then drag your cursor around the perimeter of that area. (You can

---

TIPS FOR MAKING SELECTIONS

MARQUEE TOOL:
- To reposition a selection after you have released the mouse button, select the Marquee tool, then click and hold within the selected area and drag the selection into place.
- To deactivate a selection, click outside the selection with the Marquee tool.

LASSO TOOL:
- You must end the selection where you began it (make a closed shape).
- To draw a perfectly straight horizontal or vertical line, press and hold the Shift key while you are tracing the edge of your selection.

Using the Lasso tool, the pigs were selected. Then their color was adjusted to make them blue—without changing any other portion of the image.

also used the Polygonal Lasso tool to create geometric selections or the Magnetic Lasso tool, which tries to help you make more accurate selections by automatically "sticking" to lines in the image.)

▣ MAGIC WAND

The Magic Wand is used to select areas based on their color. To use it, choose the Magic Wand from the Tool bar (see lesson 4). Identify the area to be selected. Click on one point in that area. The Magic Wand will automatically select that point and all other contiguous points of the same color. (To select all the points of the same color in the entire image, just click to deactivate the Contiguous setting in the Options bar.) By setting the Tolerance in the Options bar, you can define how picky Elements will be in defining what colors are "the same" as the one you indicated (and, therefore, what will be included in the selection). The larger the number you enter, the more liberal its definition will be. A good place to start is at about 30.

▣ SELECTION BRUSH

Another great tool is the Selection Brush. To use it, simply "paint" over the area you want to select by clicking and dragging. In the Options bar, you can choose a larger or smaller brush size and select the hardness of the brush (for more on this, see lesson 32).

30. MODIFYING SELECTIONS

I n addition to helping us when we can't trace the perfect shape with our mouse, modifying selections helps us be strategic about making selections.

■ ADDING/SUBTRACTING

To add to a selection (include more within it), choose a selection tool. In the Options bar, click on the Add to Selection icon. A "+" will appear next to your

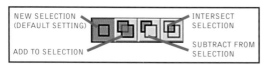

NEW SELECTION (DEFAULT SETTING)
ADD TO SELECTION
INTERSECT SELECTION
SUBTRACT FROM SELECTION

cursor. (Holding the Shift key will also set the tool to "add.") Use the tool to select the area you want to add. It's okay if the new area overlaps the previously selected areas; the overlaps will be combined in the new selection. To subtract from a selection (cut from the existing selection), choose a selection tool and click on the Subtract from Selection icon. A "–" will appear next to your cursor. Select the area you want to remove from your selection. (Holding the Opt/Alt key will also set the tool to "subtract.")

■ INVERSING

Inversing a selection (Select>Inverse) selects all of the areas that are *not* in the current selection.

■ FEATHERING

You may notice that the edges of the selected area look very hard and abrupt. Feathering a selection allows you to slightly (or dramatically) blur the edges of the selected area, creating a smoother look. To do this, go to Select>Feather

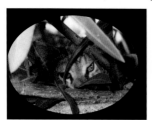  

To vignette an image (darken the corners and edges), the Marquee tool was used to select an oval in the center of the image. The selection was then inversed to select the areas outside this oval. By going to Edit>Fill (see lesson 33), the selected area was filled with black (left). The edges of the vignette looked hard, so the Undo History palette was used to undo the fill and the selection was feathered 50 pixels (center) before reapplying the Fill command. For a softer look, the Undo History palette was used again to undo the Fill command, and the selection was feathered 100 pixels before filling it again with black (right).

Making complicated selections takes some time—especially when you are new to the process. When you have finished making one, you can save it by going to Select>Save Selection. In the dialog box, name your selection and make sure New Selection is chosen. Then hit the OK button. If you need to reuse the selection, just go to Select>Load Selection and choose the selection you named from the pull-down menu at the top of the dialog box that appears.

and enter the desired value in the dialog box. The higher the value, the blurrier the edges of the selection. In general, 2 pixels will create a soft edge.

■ SELECT>MODIFY

With a selection made and still active, go to Select>Modify and choose the option you want (Border, Expand, Contract, or Smooth). In the dialog box that appears, select the degree of change by entering a number of pixels (the higher the number, the greater the change). Experimenting with the settings will give you a good idea of what to anticipate.

■ GROW

The Grow command allows you to increase an already selected area. It does this by causing the selection to include similar tones in contiguous areas. To apply the Grow command to an active selection, go to Select>Grow. You can do this repeatedly to make your selection grow incrementally larger.

■ SIMILAR

The Similar command also allows you to add to your selection. Rather than adding similar contiguous tones, the Similar command seeks out similar tones throughout the image and adds them to your selection. To use the Similar command on an active selection, go to Select>Similar.

31. WORKING WITH SELECTIONS

If you're like most photographers, you don't shoot a lot of absolutely perfect images. Most of us take a lot of good pictures—pictures we'd like a lot more if we could fix just one or two little things. When you start working with selections, you can isolate the changes you make—meaning you can adjust only the parts of the image that bother you and leave the rest alone. The following are some common operations using selections.

■ DISTRACTING BACKGROUNDS

Who doesn't have a bunch of family photos like the one below? We keep them because the subject looks good, but don't frame them because, well, nothing *else* really does. To eliminate background problems, select the background, then make whatever adjustments are needed to improve things. This could include applying filters, using the Brightness/Contrast command, using the Clone Stamp tool to stamp out problems (see lesson 35), etc. Whatever tool you want to use, you won't have to worry about messing up the subjects; the selection will constrain your changes to the background.

There's a lot of stuff in the background (left)—a trellis, part of a tent, and somebody's hat on the far right. To create the image on the right, the background was selected using the Lasso tool. The Gaussian Blur filter was used on the selected area, and its contrast and brightness were adjusted.

■ CHANGING COLORS

In lesson 20 we looked at the Hue/Saturation command, which can be used to change one color to another. By itself, this is very effective if the color you want to change appears nowhere other than where you want to change it. What happens, though, when you want to change a pink dress to a blue dress, but you don't want the pink purse to change color at the same time (top-left image, facing page)? The answer, as you have probably already guessed, is that you make a selection.

Using a selection made with the Magic Wand tool, the pink color in the dress (left) was isolated and changed to another color (right) without affecting any of the other areas of the image.

Once you've selected the area where you want to change the color, you can use whatever tool or command you want to execute the change—and it will only affect the selected area.

■ COMPOSITING IMAGES

Imagine you have two almost identical pictures of your friend. In one, she is posed in a very flattering way—but she blinked during the exposure! In the other, her eyes are open and she's showing her great smile—but she put her hand in her pocket and it doesn't look as good. To fix the problem and create one great image, you could select the head from the image where her face looks great, copy the selected area, then paste it into the image where the pose is great. This technique is called compositing (see lesson 42 for more on this).

MORE TIPS FOR WORKING WITH SELECTIONS

- To automatically create a new layer, make a selection, then go to Edit>Cut or Edit>Copy (cutting removes the area, copying duplicates it). Then, go to Edit>Paste. The material you paste will reappear on a new layer.
- When you are done with a selection, deselect it by clicking outside it with the Marquee tool or go to Select>Deselect. To reactivate your latest selection, go to Select>Reselect.

32. ADDING ARTWORK

Many of the tools in Elements are used for painting and drawing, etc. When using these tools, you need to be able to specify the color of "paint" that you want to use and the type of brush you'll use to apply it.

■ COLORS

You can keep your "brushes" loaded with two colors—the foreground and background colors. Swatches of the current setting for each color appear at the bottom of the Tool bar.

The foreground color is the color actively available for painting or drawing. When you open Elements, the foreground color will be set to black, and the background color will be set to white. However, this can be changed and set however you like.

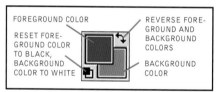

The foreground and background colors are at the bottom of the Tool bar.

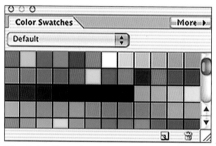

The Color Swatches.

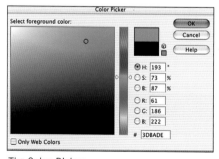

The Color Picker.

The easiest way to change the foreground color is to use the preset colors provided in the Swatches palette (Window>Color Swatches). To set one of these colors as your foreground color, simpy click on the square with the color you like. To use one of them as your background color, just hold down the ⌘/Cmd key and click on a swatch.

To create a custom color, use the Color Picker. To open it click once on either the foreground or background color swatch in the Tool bar. In the Color Picker dialog box, you will see a large window with shades of a single color. To the right is a narrow bar with the full spectrum of colors. At the top right are two swatches; at the top is the current color, and at the bottom is the original color. To use the Color Picker, begin with the narrow bar that runs through the colors of the rainbow. Click and drag either of the sliders on the bar up and down until you see something close to the color you want in the large window. Then, in that large window, move your cursor over the color you want and click to select it. Hit OK.

To select a second color, use the bent arrow above the color swatches in the Tool bar to reverse the foreground and background colors. This will swap your first color into the background so you can pick a new foreground color. Reverse these as often as you want.

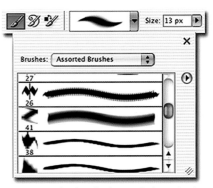

You can set the brush size and shape in the Options bar.

■ BRUSHES

When you select a painting tool (see lesson 33), the Options bar changes to include brush size and shape. You can also set the opacity (how transparent the paint you apply will be), and the mode of the paint (identical in name and function to the layer modes—see lesson 26).

To select one of the many preset brushes, click on the rectangular box with the brush stroke in it in the Options bar. At the top of the window that pops open, you can select from different types of brushes and see samples of them in the window below. To adjust the size of the brush, move to the right on the Options bar and enter a number (the larger the number, the bigger the brush). To adjust the opacity of the paint or the mode, continue to move to the right on the Options bar and set each one as you like.

When you're done, just click and drag over your image to begin painting with the foreground color you chose.

In the Options bar, click on the tool icon next the the words "More Options" to further customize your brushes by adjusting the hardness and other characteristics. Consult Elements' excellent Help files for more details on these very specialized settings.

THE EYEDROPPER

You can use the Eyedropper tool (see lesson 4) to select a color from your image to use as the foreground color. Just choose the Eyedropper from the Tool bar and click on the desired color in your image.

33. PAINTING AND FILLING

The painting tools have similar options but specialized functions, as described below. The fill tools are used to cover large areas, or to fill selected areas with a color or pattern.

■ BRUSH AND PENCIL

Select the tool, pick a brush, and set the tool options as you like. Then, click and drag over your image to paint or draw with the foreground color.

■ IMPRESSIONIST BRUSH

The Impressionist Brush adds a stylized effect to your image. To use it, you'll still select a brush, as you would with the Brush tool, but your foreground color won't matter; this tool draws its colors from your image. The more times you pass the brush over an area (or the longer you leave it over an area), the more distorted it will become.

The background was selected (ensuring the painting would not affect the subject) and the Impressionist Brush was used to distort it.

■ ERASER

Erasing the background layer removes data to let the background color show through. Erasing an overlying layer lets the underlying layer show through.

◼ SPONGE

The Sponge tool has two modes in the Options bar: Saturate (increase the color intensity) and Desaturate (decrease the color intensity). To use this tool, select the option you want, then move your brush over the image and "paint" the change over the desired area.

◼ FILL SELECTION OR LAYER

To fill an area with a color, go to Edit>Fill. If you have an active selection, it will be filled (Edit>Fill Selection); if not, the whole image area will be filled (Edit>Fill Layer). From the bottom of the Fill dialog box, you can select the fill mode and opacity (this is the same as for layers; see lesson 26). From the Contents menu, you can choose to fill with either the foreground color, the background color, black, white, 50-percent gray, or even a pattern.

Fill Layer	
💡 Learn more about: Fill Layer	OK
	Cancel
Contents	
Use: Foreground Color ⬍	
Custom Pattern: ▾	
Blending	
Mode: Normal ⬍	
Opacity: 100 %	
☐ Preserve Transparency	

The Fill Layer dialog box.

◼ PATTERNS

To fill with a pattern, go to Edit>Fill, select Pattern from the Contents menu, and click the Custom Pattern thumbnail to view the existing patterns. To create a custom pattern, close the Fill box and select an area of your image. Then, go to Edit>Define Pattern From Selection. In the dialog box that appears, name your pattern and hit OK. When you return to the Custom Pattern thumbnail in the Fill dialog box, the new pattern will be listed.

◼ PAINT BUCKET

The Paint Bucket is like a combination of the Magic Wand tool and the Fill command. To use it, set the Tolerance in the Options bar (the higher the tolerance, the more of your image the tool will paint) and click on the area you want to fill. All areas of the same color will instantly be filled with the current foreground color.

34. TEXT TOOL

To add text to an image, select the Text tool from the Tool bar, then set the options as you like. Click anywhere on your image and a blinking cursor will appear. From here, begin typing your text. When you have finished, click

The Text tool was selected and text was added to the image.

Using the Move tool, the text was dragged into position.

The Confetti type effect was added to the image, but it didn't seem right and was undone (Edit>Undo).

The text was selected by clicking and dragging over it with the Text tool. The Text Warp was applied.

the "⊘" (at the far right of the Options bar) to cancel your work or the "✓" button to accept it. Selecting a new tool will automatically accept the current text. All text is automatically created on a new layer.

■ OPTIONS

You have a number of good options for fine-tuning your text. In the Options bar, these are (left to right):

Font Style. Choose regular or another style (these vary from font to font).

Font Family. Select the style of type you wish to use.

Font Size. Select a size from the pull-down list or type in your own value.

Anti-Aliased. Smoothes the curves in the letters, preventing a jagged look.

Text Styles. Lets you bold, italicize, or underline text.

Paragraph Justification. Controls how the lines in a paragraph are aligned (left, centered, or right).

Text Color. Sets the color of the text. Click on this box to activate the Color Picker (see lesson 32).

Text Warp. Allows you to create curved and otherwise distorted text. Simply select the style of warp you want, then set it to vertical or horizontal. By adjusting the bend and horizontal/vertical distortion, you can set the warp as you like.

After undoing the Text Warp, the Water Reflection effect was selected for the final image.

Vertical or Horizontal Text.
Select whether text runs across the page or up and down it.

■ EDITING TEXT

To edit your text, select the Text tool and click on the text in your image to reactivate the cursor. Select blocks of text by clicking and dragging. You can also cut or copy and paste text by selecting it and going to Edit>Cut/Copy and Edit>Paste.

■ TEXT EFFECTS

To add some interesting effects to your text, check out the text effects in the Effects palette (see lesson 24).

■ TYPE MASK TOOL

Sometimes the effect you want to create with type is better accom-

In the top image, the word SPRING was selected using the Type Mask tool. The selected area was then copied (Edit>Copy) and pasted (Edit>Paste) into a new file (second image). It could also have been pasted into a new layer in the original leaf image or into another photo. From there, it can be customized as you would any other image layer. In the third image, a bevel was added from the Effects palette. In the final image, the Pointillize filter (Filter>Pixelate> Pointillize) was applied, and a drop shadow was added.

plished with the text as a selection rather than as editable text. To do this, go to the Tool bar and hold down on the Text tool. Then choose one of the Text as Mask tools and type your text on the layer where you want the selection to be active. An example of this is shown above.

COOKIE CUTTER

Elements offers a vast array of interesting custom shapes that you can add to your images—there are frames, animals, arrows, symbols, foods, and much more. To add a custom shape to your image, select the Cookie Cutter tool. In the Options bar, click on the Shape menu (part of which is seen here) and pick a shape. Choose the shape you want to use, then click and drag over your image to add it. You can fill the shape with a color or do anything else you want to it.

35. BASIC RETOUCHING

Professional image retouching can make a portrait subject look like a million bucks. Now the same tools pros use are at your fingertips, so you never have to live with blemishes and other little problems—even in your snapshots!

■ THE CLONE STAMP TOOL

The Clone Stamp tool works just like a rubber stamp, but the "ink" for the stamp is data from one good area of your image that you "stamp" over a problem area of your image. Using this tool definitely takes some practice, but once you master it, you'll probably find you use it on just about every image.

To begin, choose the Clone Stamp tool from the Tool bar. Then, set the brush size in the Options bar (the size you choose will depend on the area available to sample from and the area you want to cover). Move your mouse

The Clone Stamp tool is perfect for removing small blemishes (left) and creating a more flawless look (right). You can even use it to remove stray hairs and shape the eyebrows! Image by Jeff Smith.

The Red Eye Brush can be used to remove red-eye (left) and create a much more pleasing appearance (right).

over the area that you want to clone, then hold down the Opt/Alt key and click. Next, move your mouse over the area where you want the cloned data to appear and click (or click and drag). As with the other painting tools, you can also adjust the mode and opacity of the Clone Stamp tool in the Options bar. Don't forget to use the Zoom tool to enlarge your view for precise work.

■ RED EYE REMOVAL TOOL

Red-eye is just a fact of the anatomy of our eyes, but that doesn't mean we have to live with it in our images. Elements makes it easy to remove the problem and create a much more pleasant look. For this correction, it will be very helpful to zoom in tightly on the eyes you want to correct.

To use the Red Eye Removal Tool, choose it from the Tool bar, then select the brush settings you want. Click on Default Colors to reset the Current color to red and the Replacement Color to black. Then, make sure the Sampling menu is set to First Click. Position your mouse over a red area of the eye and click (or click and drag) to replace the red with a dull gray.

If the red isn't all replaced, try setting the Tolerance slider higher (the default 30-percent setting will work for almost every image, though).

To select a different Replacement Color to more accurately match the color of the subject's eyes, click on the Replacement Color swatch and choose a new color from the Color Picker.

36. SHARPENING AND SOFTENING

Sharpening and softening are everyday operations with digital images. In Elements, you can use the sharpening and softening filters to improve flaws in an image or to enhance the appearance of your subject.

■ SHARPENING

If your image looks pretty much okay, but a little fuzziness is apparent when you really get critical, sharpening may do the trick. Almost every scan of an image also requires at least a little sharpening to make it look crisp. To sharp-

en an image, go to Filter>Sharpen.

The Sharpen filter applies itself to every pixel in the image or selection, enhancing the contrast between adjoining pixels to create the appearance of sharper focus. The Sharpen More filter does the same thing, but with more intensity.

The Sharpen Edges filter looks for the edges of objects in an image and tries to enhance them to create the look of increased sharpness.

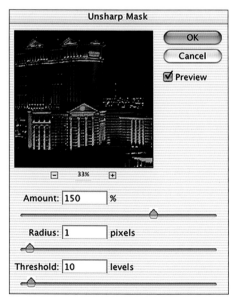

The original image (top) was scanned from a print and needed sharpening. With the Unsharp Mask (right), the image was slightly sharpened (middle). Sharpening must be done in moderation. Oversharpened photos (bottom) look grainy and have unattractive light halos around dark areas, and dark halos around light ones.

To give a softer look to the original image (left), the background layer was duplicated, slightly blurred, and set to the Lighten mode (right).

Unsharp Mask is the most powerful sharpening filter in Elements. To begin, go to Filter>Sharpen>Unsharp Mask. This will bring up a dialog box in which you can adjust the Amount (how much sharpening occurs), the Radius (how far from each pixel the effect is applied), and the Threshold (how similar in value the pixels must be to be sharpened). To start, try setting the Amount to 150 percent, the Radius to 1 or 2 pixels, and the Threshold to 10 levels. Watch the preview and fine-tune these settings until you like the results.

Watch out for oversharpening. If you're not sure you've sharpened an image correctly, go to Edit>Undo and compare the new version to the original. If the new one was better, use Edit>Redo to return to it.

◼ SOFTENING

Images from digital cameras are often so amazingly sharp that they just don't make people look their best (who wants to see every flaw on their skin?).

To add a forgiving amount of softness, duplicate the background layer and apply the Gaussian Blur filter to it (Filter>Blur>Gaussian Blur) at a low setting (3–5 pixels). After applying the filter, set the mode of the duplicated layer to Lighten (at the top of the Layers palette).

The result with be a soft, light glow that makes many subjects look better— and not just people. You can use this effect on any scene where you want a more gentle feeling.

37. DODGING AND BURNING

Original photograph (top). The photo with 20-percent exposure dodge on the midtones (bottom).

Ansel Adams was a master in the photographic darkroom, and two of the techniques he used are simulated by these tools. While mastering them may not make you a legendary photographer, it will definitely help you make the most of your images.

■ DODGING

The Dodge tool is used to lighten areas of an image. To use it, select the Dodge tool from the Tool bar, then choose a brush (a soft brush works best). Click (or click and drag) over your image to dodge (lighten) as needed.

In the Options bar, increasing the Exposure setting will increase the amount of lightening you achieve. In the Range menu, you can specify whether you want to lighten the shadows, midtones, or highlights in a given area. This is an important decision, so study the area you are working on carefully to determine the best approach. Often, the best selection is counterintuitive. For example, imagine you have a photo with a dark shadow area. It's not solid black but has very dark gray details. To bring out the details, it might seem logical to dodge the shadows. However, this would mean lightening the black areas—making them gray. If the shadow area and its details are *both* gray, then the contrast between them has actually been reduced—making the details even less visible. Instead, you would want to dodge the midtones, to lighten the areas that were originally dark gray. Making those gray areas a little lighter will make them more apparent to the viewer.

In the first photograph (left), the background was hazy and too light—especially when considered in comparison to the foreground. To fix this, the Burn tool was used to darken the area, balancing it better with the foreground, as seen in the final photograph (right).

■ BURNING

The Burn tool is used to darken areas of an image. To use it, select the Burn tool from the Tool bar, then choose a brush (a soft brush works best). Click (or click and drag) over your image to burn (darken) as needed.

In the Options bar, increasing the Exposure setting will increase the amount of darkening you achieve. In the Range menu, you can choose to darken the shadows, midtones, or highlights in a given area. This is an important decision, so study the area you are working on to determine the best approach. Again, the best selection may be counterintuitive. For example, imagine you have a photograph with a bright highlight area. The area is not solid white but has very light gray details. To bring out the details, it seems it would be logical to burn the highlights. However, in this case, burning the highlight areas would mean darkening the white areas—making them light gray.

If the highlight area and its details are both light gray, then the contrast between them has actually been reduced—making the details even less visible. Instead, you would want to burn the midtones or shadows to make the areas that were originally light gray become somewhat darker. This will make them more apparent to the viewer of the image.

38. LIQUIFYING IMAGES

The Liquify filter (Filter>Distort>Liquify) deserves some special considera-
tion when discussing methods for retouching and refining photos, because
it allows you to freely twist, stretch, and warp an image.

While warping may not sound like an operation that would fall under the
category of retouching, it actually does. As you can see below and on the facing page, selectively distorting small areas of an image can help to eliminate
little figure flaws in portraits for a more flattering look. It can also be used to
smooth out the little bulges that result from tight clothing, like snug waist-
bands. In advertising photography, this tool is even used to make a model's
eyes or lips look a little bigger or more full.

The key to using the tool for retouching is subtlety. The more you distort
a given area, the more likely the refinement will look fake. When using it on
people, be careful not to distort your subjects so much that they don't look
like themselves.

To use this filter, go to Filter>Distort>Liquify. Doing so will open a full-
screen dialog box with a large preview of your image in the center and two
control panels on either side. To the left of your image are the tools, and to
the right are the options.

The Warp tool in the Liquify filter was used to slightly slim the woman's hip area for a more flattering look (left, original; right, retouched). Photo by Jeff Smith.

The man's chin and neck area (left) were reshaped using the Liquify filter (center). Using the Burn tool, the shadows were enhanced to further reduce the visibility of this area (right). Note that the change is subtle—people should still look like themselves after the correction. Photo by Jeff Smith.

To begin, select the Warp, Turbulence, Twist, Pucker, Bloat, Shift Pixels, or Reflection tool. Then, choose a brush from the Options bar. For the most impact, select a rather large brush (perhaps in the 50–100 range), and set the brush pressure to about 50 (higher settings will provide even more distortion). Then, by clicking and dragging over the image preview, simply begin painting on the distortion. The longer you leave your brush in one area, the more the pixels there will be distorted. Try experimenting with several of the tools, using different brush sizes and pressures, and painting quickly versus slowly.

If you like the results shown in the preview window, hit OK to accept the changes. If you don't like them but you want to try again, hit Revert.

Of course, the Liquify filter can also be used to create effects that are far from natural!

39. PHOTO PROJECT: HANDCOLORING

Handcoloring photos is traditionally accomplished with a variety of artistic media—oil paints, pencils, etc. With Elements, you can create this classic look much more easily!

■ METHOD 1

This technique gives you total control over the colors you add and where you add them.

1. Open an image. If it's a color image, go to Enhance>Adjust Color> Remove Color to create a black & white image. If it's a black & white image, go on to the next step.

2. Create a new layer and set it to the Color mode (see lesson 26).

3. Click on the foreground color swatch to activate the Color Picker. Select the color you want and hit OK.

4. With your color selected, return to the new layer you created in your image. Click on this layer in the Layers palette to activate it, and make sure that it is set to the Color mode.

5. Select the Brush tool and whatever size/hardness brush you like, then begin painting. Because you have set the layer mode to color, the color you apply with the brush will allow the underlying photo to show through.

6. If you're a little sloppy, use the Eraser tool (set to 100 percent in the Options bar) to remove the color from anywhere you didn't mean to put it.

The original image (left). The image handcolored using method 1 (right).

The original image (left). The image handcolored using method 2 (right).

Using the Zoom tool to move in tight on these areas will help you work as precisely as possible.

7. If you want to add more than one color, you may wish to use more than one layer, all set to the Color mode.

8. When you've completed the "handcoloring," your image may be either completely or partially colored. With everything done, you can flatten the image and save it as you like.

■ METHOD 2

Here's a quick way to add a handcolored look in seconds—or, with a little refinement, to avoid having to select colors to handcolor with. This technique works only if you are starting with a color image.

1. Begin by duplicating the background layer (by dragging it onto the duplication icon at the top of the Layers palette).

2. Next, remove the color from the background copy by going to Enhance> Adjust Color>Remove Color. The image will turn black & white—but by reducing the opacity of the new layer you can allow the colors from the underlying photo to show through as much or as little as you like.

3. To create the look of a more traditional black & white handcolored image, set the opacity of the desaturated layer to 100 percent and use the Eraser tool to reveal the underlying photo. Adjust the Eraser's opacity to allow as much color to show through as you like.

4. For a very soft look, set the opacity of the desaturated layer to about 90 percent (just enough to let colors show through faintly) and use the Eraser tool (set to about 50 percent) to erase areas where you want an accent of stronger color to appear.

40. PHOTO PROJECT: IMAGE RESTORATION

The first step when restoring an image is to make a quick visual analysis and create a to-do list of things to fix. For this image, the list included: removing small spots and specks, repairing the torn corner and crease, removing an ink mark, and improving the color and contrast.

The first step was to correct the various spots scattered across the photograph. To do this, the Clone Stamp tool was used to sample nearby data and copy it over the damaged areas.

Next, an undamaged area of the background was selected with the Marquee tool. This was copied and pasted, then moved (with the Move tool) over the torn edge. The missing areas were then filled in using the same method. The Clone Stamp tool was then used to disguise any edges that were visible.

The crease across the image was also fixed using the Clone Stamp tool, as was the ink mark at the bottom of the photograph (as you can see, this is a pretty useful tool!). With areas like these where there is a lot of texture and image detail, it's important to zoom in and use a small brush to do your work. The areas you sample with your tool should also be selected very carefully to

The original image (left) had a torn corner, a crease, an ink mark, and some yellow discoloration. After removing some spots and specks, part of the background was copied and used to begin repairing the torn corner (right).

ensure they will blend seamlessly over the area that you want to conceal.

Finally, the Auto Color command (Enhance>Auto Color Correction) was used to eliminate the color cast. If you wanted to keep the faded sepia color, you could skip this step—or you could remove the color cast as suggested and then use the technique in lesson 20 to add a customized toning effect.

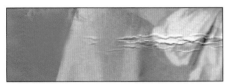

The crease was repaired using the Clone Stamp tool. Zooming in (top left) ensured accurate corrections. After fixing the torn corner and crease, the ink mark still needed to be removed (top right). This was also done with the Clone Stamp tool (bottom left). Finally, the Auto Color Correction command was employed to remove the color cast.

41. PHOTO PROJECT: PANORAMIC IMAGES

Panoramic images are created digitally by shooting a sequence of images and then combining them into one photograph.

■ SHOOTING THE IMAGES

If you want to make a panoramic image, you'll need to plan to do so *before* you start shooting.

Whether you shoot film or digital, you'll want to select a mid-range lens (neither telephoto nor wide angle)—this would be about a 50mm lens on a 35mm camera. If you are using a point-and-shoot with a zoom lens, set it about halfway out. It might seem like a good idea to use a wide-angle lens for panoramics, but this will cause distortion at the edges of images, making them impossible to join together seamlessly.

When you start shooting, select one exposure setting and focus setting and stick to it. The idea is to create the impression of a single image, and that won't happen if some sections are lighter/darker than others, or if the focus suddenly shifts from the foreground to the background.

It's also important to maintain a consistent camera height (for best results, use a tripod and rotate the camera as you take each shot).

Let's imagine you are standing facing the part of the scene that you want to have on the left edge of your final panoramic. Lift the camera and take the first shot, noting what is on the right-hand edge of the frame. Pivot slightly to the right and place the subject matter that was in the right-hand part of the first frame just inside the left edge of the second photo. Continue this process until you've taken enough images to cover the desired area. Ideally, you should have about a 10–20 percent overlap between the images.

If you're shooting digitally, check to see if your camera has a panoramic setting. If so, switching it to this setting will usually change the display on the

LCD screen so that you can see the image you are about to shoot and the previous image side-by-side, making it easy to set up each successive shot.

■ PHOTOMERGE

Once you've shot the images, combining them is a relatively simple procedure. When you go to File>New>Photomerge Panorama the first window will open. Click Browse and select the images you want to merge. When all of the files appear in the Source Files window, hit OK and watch things start to happen.

When the second Photomerge window appears, Elements will try to place all of the photos in the correct position. If it can't, it will let you know. If this happens, the photos it can't place will appear as thumbnails at the top of the window. You can then drag them down into the main window and position them yourself. You can also click and drag the other images in the main window to reposition them if Elements doesn't do it correctly. When everything is in position, hit OK.

When the final image appears, it may have some uneven edges where the original photos overlap. Cropping the image will eliminate this and create the impression of a single image.

42. PHOTO PROJECT: COMPOSITING IMAGES

These images meet the criteria for compositing.

Originally, one of the most interesting uses for digital imaging was to combine elements of two images in a realistic way. While it's no longer a *primary* reason to use digital, compositing can still be a fun exercise.

For realistic results, the direction and quality of lighting should be very similar in both photos. It also helps if all of the elements are well exposed and have no big color problems. Check to make sure the focus is correct; a softly focused subject in a sharply focused group won't look realistic.

Look at the images carefully and decide which contains more of the material you want in the final image. In this case, the theater (top) will be the background. The only part of the other image that will be used is the figure in the center of the frame (bottom).

Therefore, the woman was selected, and the selection was then feathered to soften the edges and make them less obvious when moving the subject into the theater image. The selected area was copied (Edit>Copy) and pasted (Edit>Paste) into a new layer in the theater image.

Correct positioning of the new element on the new layer was the next task. To do this accurately, look at the scale of the imported material. Does it need to be changed in order to make sense with the subjects around it? Then, think about perspective. If your background image (as here) shows a scene in the distance, the subject must be at a correct size in relation to its apparent distance from the camera. In the images at the top of the facing page, you can see the difference between reasonably good perspective and an obviously wrong one. In each image, the figure size remained the same; only the position changed.

Next, look at the color, brightness, and contrast of the new element in relation to the background image. Correct any problems using the Levels command or one of the other image-adjustment controls.

With the image almost complete, the only thing obviously missing was the woman's shadow. Everything else in the image has long, dark shadows; adding one to the woman enforced the realism of the effect.

To add the shadow, the layer containing the subject was duplicated in the Layers palette. After activating the new layer, the Brightness/Contrast control (see lesson 19) was set to –100 on both sliders, making the subject go black on this layer.

Good placement.   Bad placement.

Next, the Image>Transform> Distort command was used to drag the top of the new layer down diagonally, matching the angle of the other shadows in the scene. The shadow needed to bend up onto a wall, so a second selection was made of the area of the shadow that would go up the wall. The Distort function was then used again to bend the shadow appropriately.

The shadow is distorted to match other shadows in the scene.   The top of the shadow was selected and distorted to run up the wall.

With the basic outline of the shadow in place, the Gaussian Blur filter (set to 5 pixels) was used to create a softer edge on the shadow. The final step was to make the shadow more transparent by reducing the opacity of the layer it was on. In this case, the opacity was set to 30 percent.

Final composited image.

43. IMAGES IN ACTION

What's the point in creating a great image if you don't display it well? It is important to make sure your images look their best as you show them off, whether in prints on online.

■ IMAGE PREP

Before outputting, flatten any layers you have created. Then, save the image in the required file format (usually JPEG or TIFF). Finally, double-check the size and resolution of your image.

■ PRINTING

When printing on your inkjet printer, check the manual for the resolution it recommends and to learn about the printer's software. If it allows you to choose, be sure to select the setting that best matches your paper. For best results, try printing on digital photo paper.

Lab printing is really a win–win situation. The prints are real photographs that look better than inkjet prints and will last years longer. Also, they actually cost *less* than printing at home. For online photo labs (like www.Snapfish .com and www.Shutterfly.com), save your files as JPEGs and upload them directly to the website. To use a lab in your area, save your files as JPEGs on CD (or on a digital memory card) and just take them to the lab.

■ PICTURE PACKAGES

The Picture Package function (File>Picture Package) lets you print multiple copies of one image in an arrangement of sizes on one page. For home printing, this is especially efficient, since it allows you to make the most of each sheet you print.

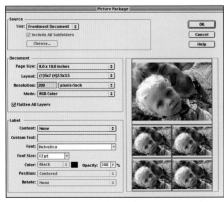

The Picture Package dialog box.

■ SLIDE SHOWS

To create a slide show, go to File> Automation Tools>PDF Slideshow. From the dialog box, select the photos for your slide show, how long each remains on-screen, and how to transition between them. Under Output File, click Choose to select a name for your slide show, then hit OK. To view the slide show, use Adobe Acrobat (download it for free at www.adobe.com).

■ WEB PHOTO GALLERY

The Web Photo Gallery software in Elements lets you create a web page to display your photos. To start, move the photos you want on your page to one folder. Then, go to File>Create Web Photo Gallery and choose the gallery style from the pull-down menu (there are many to choose from). Enter your e-mail address if you want it to appear on the page, then (under Folders) select the folder of images for your page and choose a place to save the page. When you've completed your web photo gallery, you can view it on your computer or upload it to your web site.

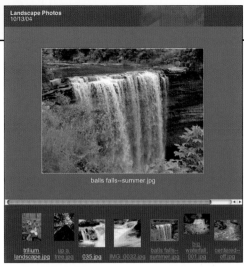

The Web Photo Gallery lets you create a web page to display your photos.

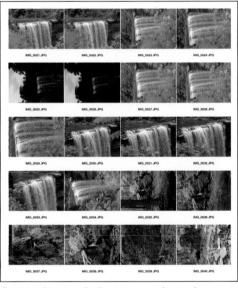

Contact sheets make it easy to track your images.

■ CONTACT SHEETS

When you start working digitally, you'll probably take more images than you ever did with film. This sheer volume of images can make it tough to find a particular image when you want it. To make this easier, it's very useful to create contact sheets (File>Print Layouts>Contact Sheet). This lets you print lots of small images on one page and automatically puts the name of the file under each one. As you archive your work to CD-R or DVD-R, try to make a contact sheet for each disc and store it with the disc.

AFTERWORD

As you can see, Adobe Photoshop Elements is an extremely powerful tool. Having read this book and learned the techniques covered in it, you have the knowledge to complete just about any imaging project you can dream up. This doesn't mean that you're done learning or that you'll never get frustrated (or completely puzzled). You will—*everyone* does. Elements is a complex program that takes some practice to master.

Fortunately, gaining experience in Elements is a lot of fun—just find some images and put your imagination to work. You may also want to keep your eyes open for digital effects we see every day in the photos on billboards, in magazines, on television, etc.—then try to replicate the effect yourself with your own images.

As you expand your experience with the tools that are covered in this book, don't be afraid to check out some of the other features and functions. The worst that can happen is that you make your image look terrible and have to go to Edit>Undo. Ultimately, that is the very best part of digital imaging—you can experiment to your heart's content and almost never need to start over. Good luck!

INDEX

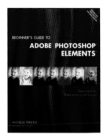

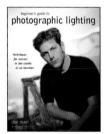

PROFESSIONAL TECHNIQUES FOR
BLACK & WHITE DIGITAL PHOTOGRAPHY
Patrick Rice

Black & white photography is an enduring favorite among photographers—and digital imaging now makes it easier than ever to create this classic look. From shooting techniques to refining your images in the new digital darkroom, this book is packed with step-by-step techniques (including tips for black & white digital infrared photography) that will help you achieve dazzling results! $29.95 list, 8½x11, 128p, 100 color photos, index, order no. 1798.

PORTRAIT PHOTOGRAPHER'S HANDBOOK,
2nd Ed.
Bill Hurter

Bill Hurter, editor of *Rangefinder* magazine, presents a step-by-step guide to professional-quality portraiture. The reader-friendly text easily leads you through all phases of portrait photography, while images from the top professionals in the industry provide ample inspiration. This book will be an asset to experienced photographers and beginners alike. $29.95 list, 8½x11, 128p, 175 color photos, order no. 1708.

OUTDOOR AND LOCATION
PORTRAIT PHOTOGRAPHY, 2nd Ed.
Jeff Smith

With its ever-changing light conditions, outdoor portrait photography can be challenging—but it can also be incredibly beautiful. Learn to work with natural light, select locations, and make all of your subjects look their very best. This book is packed with illustrations and step-by-step discussions to help you achieve professional results! $29.95 list, 8½x11, 128p, 80 color photos, index, order no. 1632.